Praise for *As Yourself*

"In these harsh times, Caroline Vogel invites us to cultivate grace as an embodied practice. At once reflective and practical, *As Yourself* re-orients us to the ancient call to love our neighbors as ourselves."

—**Stephanie Paulsell,** Susan Shallcross Swartz Professor of the Practice of Christian Studies, Emerita
Harvard Divinity School

"With tenderness and clarity, Vogel invites us to receive our belovedness until, at last, we feel it settle into our bellies and sink into the marrow of our bones. *As Yourself* is an exquisite book about becoming living, breathing expressions of divine love, grounded in grace and enlivened by the sacredness of our own humanity."

—**Bonnie Smith Whitehouse**,
author of *In Our Hands* and *Seasons of Wonder*

"In sharing her own journey and wisdom, Caroline offers us an invitation to slow down, to listen, to love. She has done and is doing the work of living into the fullness of an integrated mind, body, and spirit and offers a reminder that we are enough, just as we are, and that we are forever unfolding in the mystery of grace."

—**Cami Twilling,** Director, Earth & Soul

"Vogel tenderly weaves theology, embodiment, and self-compassion in a way that honors trauma, names grace as relational, and affirms that loving God and neighbor is inseparable from learning to love ourselves. This book is a gift to anyone seeking a faith-rooted, emotionally honest path toward healing, dignity, and holy self-acceptance."

—**Ragan Schriver**, PsyD, MSW, Clinical Professor in the College of Social Work at the University of Tennessee; Vicar, St. Luke's Episcopal Church, Knoxville, TN

"Caroline's insightful interpretations of Biblical stories, instructions for mindful breathing meditations, and purposefully constructed prayers are a loving open door to any who seek the fruit of the spirit."

—**Miranda Clark,** Librarian, The Episcopal School of Knoxville, TN

"Loving ourselves as much as we love others is one of the most difficult, yet essential, dilemmas on our journey to our authentic selves. Through personal stories and essential practices, Caroline helps us not only read about loving ourselves but gives us practical ways to do it."

—**The Reverend Canon Thom Rasnick,**
Sub-Dean, St. John's Episcopal Cathedral

"I cherish this book for the way it illuminates what Jesus meant when he commanded us to love our neighbors *as ourselves*. Caroline's embodied wisdom invites us to receive the grace that Christ has already placed within our very cells."

—**Elizabeth B. Strand**, Ph.D., LCSW, One Health Chaplain

"*As Yourself* is an invitation to grow your Christian faith from conceptual beliefs to embodied practices. Familiar scriptures and theological concepts are translated into a deepening self-awareness and a growing capacity for authentic, loving relationships. Human warmth and sage wisdom are often strangers, but in this book they dance together with beauty and grace."

—**Allen Proctor,** Director Emeritus, The Haden Institute

"Whether you struggle to believe that you are loved just as you are or you've long been drinking from the bottomless well of grace, Caroline's stories, dreams, insights, and practices will lead you deeper into relationship with the One who makes all things new."

—**Rev. Jen Brothers,** founder of
House of Bread and Church of the Acorn Hope

"What a fresh and much-needed reminder of the greatest commandment! Vogel offers a gentle yet firm nudge, reminding us that loving God and our neighbors also requires caring for ourselves. I can't wait to share this book with my congregation!"

—**Rev. Dr. Meredith Loftis,** PC(USA), Knoxville, TN

"*As Yourself* is a soft embrace for anyone who has struggled to offer themselves the same loving kindness God longs to offer us. Truly, these words serve as a lit candle for those of us who are lost in the darkness of self doubt and criticism."

—**Rev. Kori Robins**, United Methodist Clergy & Wellness Coach

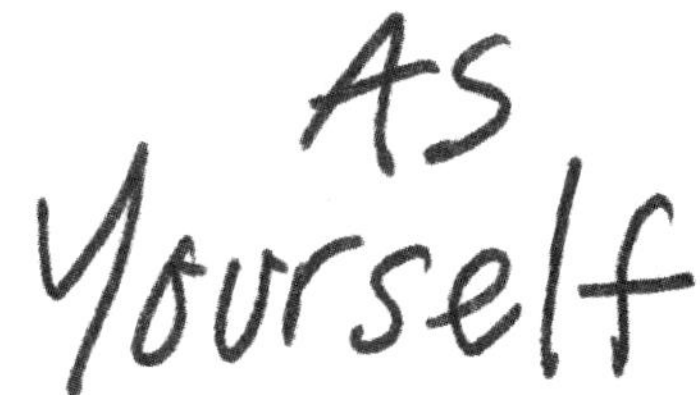

The Sacred Work of Embodying Grace

Caroline Vogel

AS YOURSELF: The Sacred Work of Embodying Grace

At the time of publication, all websites referenced in this book were valid. However, due to the fluid nature of the Internet, some addresses may have changed or the content may no longer be relevant.

Cover design: Faceout Studio
Interior design: PerfecType | Nashville, TN

ISBN: 978-0-8358-2078-3
Ebook ISBN: 978-0-8358-2079-0

Printed in the United States of America.

For more information on resources available from The Upper Room
call 1-800-972-0433 or visit www.upperroom.org

Dedicated to Andy, Aidan, & Shep
with whom I am living embodied love
imperfectly and passionately.

to Carrie, Marty, Bonnie B., Bonnie S.W.,
Sara-Scott, Gale, and Paige
who held the light of hope as I found my way into the circle of grace
and continue to be the embodiment of God's love in my life.

and to Elizabeth S. and Rara
who the Spirit showed that this book would be made manifest.

TABLE OF CONTENTS

PROLOGUE

The way of grace isn't an easy road to take, and yet it is a way of living mightily by the breath of the Spirit and into her fruit: love, joy, peace, patience, kindness, generosity, faithfulness, gentleness, and equanimity. Grace isn't only something we contemplate; grace is also an embodied practice. Grace itself is an invitation from our loving God that can be integrated and embodied in us so that such grace flows through our beings.

This book is a journey into understanding the way of loving ourselves as God loves us—in mind, body, soul, and spirit—as a pathway into living embodied grace. Bring yourself just as you are. Start wherever you find yourself today. God will meet you there. Each chapter will end with a practice and prayer so that you can begin the intention of embodiment yourself. You might simply engage the practices as they arise at the end of each chapter. You may want to engage a practice each time you pick up the book to read. Or you may want to begin to weave these practices into your everyday life.

I use the feminine pronoun for the Holy Spirit for several reasons. *Spirit* in Greek is feminine. The Holy Spirit is also known as the "Advocate," "giver of life," "helper," along with other names, and these are also gendered terms in Greek and Hebrew. Given that either pronoun can be used for the Spirit, I tend to use *she* more regularly for The Holy Spirit to diversify the predominantly male usage when referring to Jesus and God. If we are all created in God's image (Genesis 1:27), the Trinity makes room for a female reflection of the divine image.

I don't think the Trinity is all male or all female: I believe there is room for diversity in the Trinity. I'm advocating for balance and integration, for the inclusion of all people to be reflected in how we understand a triune God, because how we view God is how we often view humanity. If we struggle to see equality in our understanding of a loving God, we naturally struggle to not only see but treat and appreciate humanity with equality. When the Trinity is seen only as reflecting the masculinity of God, numerous people can feel closed off from the Trinity because they do not feel a sense of belonging. Why keep knocking when there is clearly no seat at the table for someone who looks like me? I deeply believe in a God who strives to love, connect, and serve all of creation. I find myself with new reasons to call the Holy Spirit *she* all the time, and I delight in every one of them.

So, welcome to the road and the gateways we'll pass through by the grace of a loving, benevolent God and the breath of a life-giving Spirit.

CHAPTER ONE

Love Your Neighbor as Yourself

He said to him, "'You shall love the Lord your God with all your heart and with all your soul and with all your mind.' This is the greatest and first commandment. And a second is like it: 'You shall love your neighbor as yourself.'"

MATTHEW 22:37-39

Several years ago, I was going through a particularly difficult time. My life had taken so many quick, tight turns that my nervous system, mind, body, soul, and spirit were struggling to keep up. During this time, I had to step back and reassess many aspects of my life.

One late summer night, I had a dream about my dream home. For years, I had been going to this particular home in my dreams. My dream home had large, beautiful windows that natural light poured through, cream-colored walls, cozy chairs for reading, a warm and welcoming kitchen (for someone else) to cook in, and a perfect little writing nook. Every time the Spirit led me there in my dreams, it was a divine gift.

This particular night in the dream, I was taking an evening walk with my two sons, and I realized we were in the neighborhood of my dream home. I pointed out the home to them, only to realize the house had been torn down. Even though I was surprised and hurt, I was also not totally shocked. I sensed God calling me to sit on a bench beside the foundation of this house that was once a home, and so I did. As the dream continued and I sat on the bench, God taught me about the home we were going to build together. God kept emphasizing the foundation. I began to realize that the foundation for this new house was an understanding of how to love myself as God loved me.

I recognized the dream as a symbol of God tearing down what I thought I had or wanted, leaving space to create something new and more solid in its place. This dream was a holy invitation to co-create with God an intentional home with a strong foundation of God's love that I could return to in any and every moment. I thought I understood God's love, but my dream helped me realize that this understanding had not permeated my entire being. Even though I believed in God's love and preached about it from every pulpit I could find, following the Spirit as best I could, I was not living with an embodied faith and integrated knowledge of God's love. God was calling me to allow the faith of my mind to move into the very fibers of my being and infuse my body, soul, spirit, and heart.

Given the synchronicity of life, I had an appointment with my spiritual director the morning I awoke from this dream. There at her kitchen table, we broke banana bread and leaned into the Spirit's wisdom that poured from my dream. I knew God was speaking to me in this dream. I knew God was calling me home in a new way. God had something to teach me about actually embodying the grace I professed with my lips. My spiritual director helped me see that I needed time to be with God to learn what it meant to lay a strong foundation for an inner home, a foundation of love and forgiveness, truth and healing, strength and lightness of being. Building this new "home" with God would be the process of learning to love myself as God loves me.

Just as I was getting anxious about the path before me, I realized that the Holy Spirit would be my guide. The Spirit would breathe into me her breath and guide me. As I have journeyed in this process, I have realized that the Spirit has been with me every breath, every step. I sit on the bench alongside my new foundation as it is laid by the work of the Spirit in me. I have come to know that her breath is infinitely connected to my own—the Divine breath is always breathing in us whether we are paying attention or not. Over time, I've realized that I am coming home to myself, to my own soul. Who knew it could be such a long journey to come home to one's own heart, mind, soul, spirit, body?

Drawing Myself into the Circle of Grace

The foundation God was trying to build within me revolved around learning to accept that all people are beloved children of God, which meant I had to include myself. I had to take my place within the circle of grace. I could no longer leave myself outside the circle.

Though my words would have told you that I did draw myself within the circle of God's grace, even a cursory look at my actions and self-talk proved a very different placement: a clear delineation of myself *outside* the circle of God's love. I berated myself for every misspoken word to my children and for the tone I took with them that made me inwardly cringe. I replayed conversations in my head, clearly believing that any relationship misstep would doom the friendship. I worked excessive hours, justifying it to myself because "I love what I do," when underneath the drive was a belief that I was unworthy of rest. I could not be okay with myself if I was not producing all the time. My view of myself clearly lacked any semblance of self-love or grace.

"Throwaway" Words

When Jesus was asked which commandment in the law is greatest, he replied, "'You shall love the Lord your God with all your heart and with all your soul and with all your mind' . . . and a second is like it: 'You shall love your neighbor as yourself.'" (Matt. 22:37-39). The words Jesus uses when telling listeners about the greatest commandment are words he would have learned as a child and repeated throughout his life. These words come from Deuteronomy 6:5—"You shall love the Lord your God with all your heart and with all your soul and with all your might." Jesus adds a second commandment, pulling this time from Leviticus

19:18, saying it is like the first: "love your neighbor as yourself." We are called to love God with all of our being, and we are called to love our neighbors—*as ourselves*. We talk a lot in the church about loving God and loving our neighbors, but we do a horrendous job of learning and practicing what it really means to love ourselves.

Over the years, I have chuckled at this instruction to love our neighbors as ourselves. It feels like "as yourself" is a throwaway phrase tacked on at the end of the sentence, something to which no one is really paying attention. I have heard countless preachers offer thoughts about loving God and loving your neighbor, yet make no mention of "as yourself." Jesus could have stopped the sentence early and said, "love your neighbors"—period. But he did not. He shared the whole phrase from the Hebrew scriptures: love your neighbor *as yourself*.

Perhaps loving yourself was a better understood concept in Jesus' day, and over the generations, we have lost our capacity to love ourselves because it caused us to become too vulnerable. Or maybe we've always struggled with the capacity to love ourselves, which is why Jesus kept it in the greatest commandment. Without a daily practice of loving ourselves, we will fail miserably at loving others. The more we can genuinely love ourselves as God loves us, the easier it is to naturally love others. And if there is one thing this world needs more of it is a larger capacity and willingness to practice and offer genuine love for each other.

Some will be appalled at the idea of genuinely loving ourselves. A voice in me even revolts and fears that self-love will lead to selfishness. I'm certainly not promoting narcissism. Narcissism and genuinely loving ourselves could not be further from each other. Narcissism is demanding love and attention from other people because we do not love ourselves or know how to receive God's love. When we become narcissistic, we demand from other people what we cannot or will not offer ourselves: love and belonging. Jesus' greatest commandment says that the key to loving others is learning how to love ourselves, not selfishly or narcissistically, rather as a gateway to understanding the full value of every single person, ourselves included.

"As Yourself"

The theology of "as yourself" is boldly proclaimed from the description of Maundy Thursday, according to the Gospel of John. On the night before he died, Jesus made the disciples very uncomfortable by washing their feet. Peter boldly protested that, as their teacher and superior, Jesus could not take the role of a servant and wash their feet. You can imagine Peter squirming away from Jesus' hands. However, their discomfort shook them awake and brought them to the gift of the present moment: they were physically experiencing the love of God in the touch and care of God's son. On his knees, taking the role of a servant, Jesus was laying a foundation of lived experience, an embodiment of God's love that no one could ever take from them. Later when he had died and was resurrected, even later when he ascended to be with God, the disciples could go back to that felt sense of being loved through God's touch. The mind may play tricks on us all day long, but the body does not lie.

When Jesus stood up after washing their feet, he gave them a new mandate, "love one another. Just as I have loved you, you also should love one another. By this everyone will know that you are my disciples, if you have love for one another" (John 13:34-35). Jesus could have said so many things that night. He was trying to sum up his whole earthly existence, his whole reason for becoming the embodiment of God in the first place. And there it is in two sentences. "Just as I have loved you, you also should love one another. By this everyone will know that you are my disciples, if you have love for one another."

"As yourself" is the part of the greatest commandment that so much of humanity can't grasp. Because we can't grasp it, Jesus reframes the mandate. He says, "Love one another as I have loved you." If we are ever going to figure out how to love God and our neighbors, we're going to have to risk the vulnerability of receiving God's love into our own beings. We're going to have to open ourselves to the vulnerability of being so deeply loved by God that it changes everything about us. Only when we receive God's love can we fully follow the commandment to love God and others.

For me, coming home to myself in God's love meant accepting that I couldn't earn God's love, nor would I ever fully deserve it. Hustling for God's love and for human love was killing me, and it had no place in living embodied grace. Brené Brown uses the word *hustle* to talk about how we try to outrun shame. Rather than embracing the parts of ourselves and pieces of our stories that cause us pain and tap shame, we hustle. In our hustle, we strive mightily in our own will rather than allow ourselves the vulnerability of surrendering to God's love. When we surrender, we not only accept the painful parts of our stories and lives but also open to the flow of God's love that has the power to heal and transform us. In the surrender, healing and transformation reorient our whole lives; we become integrated by grace and empowered to then live out of that grace.

Embodying grace requires that our thoughts descend from the mind into the heart and then radiate to every fiber and cell of our beings. Embodying grace means that the way I speak to myself and others, my actions toward myself and others reflects that I am a child of God who is deeply loved and cherished by the Creator. Embodying grace demands that I accept and live as if every thought, action, and attitude points to the reality that I am God's beloved.

In fact, my hustling behavior was a sign that I was outside the flow of the Spirit, outside the fullness of God's love, continuing to draw myself outside the circle of grace. Living embodied grace meant embracing the invitation to be forgiven for all the ways I drift from God's love, fail to love others, and the numerous ways I fall short of loving myself. Embodying grace meant noticing and harnessing the movement of the Holy Spirit in my life, whether she was enlightening my mind, stirring my heart, or yoking my will to God's will. All of it was grace. It was a matter of learning how to embody it.

I have struggled all my life with the idea of receiving God's love into my own being, coming home to myself in the love of God. For most of my life, I would not have told you I struggled with grace because, for the longest time, I didn't know that grace was what I was struggling with. My lips would have told you that I lived by grace. I believed in grace. Grace is the cornerstone of the Christian faith—my faith. I would not have been lying. But my lived theology—the way I lived and moved and had my being in the world—told a different story than the faith of my lips.

I heard someone say that you cannot give what you don't have. The Holy Spirit got ahold of me with this comment. "Well, what in the world have I been giving all this time?" I wondered. "What in the world was fueling my offering of love and grace to others?" It took me a long time to see it. Likely it took me a long time to be strong enough to see it because the truth was painful. I had been hustling for love and a sense of belonging. I was so eager to give other people the very thing I wanted in secret (unconscious) hope that they would reciprocate and offer love and a deep and abiding sense of belonging back to me.

Here is what the Holy Spirit has taught me: until I could be at home in myself (this vessel that God gave me), until I could love myself exactly as I am, as God loves me, and for who I am as God created me (weaknesses, flaws, imperfections and all), I'm not really loving others out of God's love. On some level, I'm simply hustling for love.

I had to learn that true love is given without restrictions, ties, or expectations. It is freely given without the need for return or interest. True love is an organic outward flow of the love God has graciously, extravagantly, abundantly given us and asked us to share with others. Given this grounding in God's love, God requires an open stance to receive love as well. True love is a natural flow of giving *and* receiving.

The Linchpin of Our Faith

The linchpin to living a life of faith isn't only about loving God and our neighbor. Both of these are only authentically possible when we allow God's love to penetrate us, breaking open our ability to love ourselves. From this wellspring of loving ourselves like God loves us, an organic outflow of God's love pours from us, transforming the way we live, breathe, work, parent, and love those around us.

We must undertake a journey to loving God and loving our neighbor by another way. This journey asks us, by the grace of God, to find, remember, and then cultivate God's deep and abiding love within us—first—so that then we love God and love others as an outpouring of our love for ourselves. The essence of our faith is already within us. It's a matter of having the courage to come home and bravely live from that authentic place of wholeness and divine love already dwelling within and ready to spill over and flow from our beings.

In our hyperfocus on loving God and loving our neighbors, what if we've missed the linchpin of faith? What if what cultivates our capacity to naturally and truly love God and love our neighbors is our ability by God's grace to love ourselves as Christ loves us? Jesus offered us the New Commandment "to love one another as I have loved you." When we can truly allow ourselves to be loved by God and receive that life-giving love, it transforms the way we live the first and second commandment—loving God and loving neighbor *as yourself*.

Most of us struggle to love God and our neighbors because we are clueless and ill-practiced in loving ourselves as Christ loves us. Most of us would rather not be loved *as yourself*, listening to the way we speak and treat ourselves. Our work as people of faith is to become willing to receive the love of God and allow that love to transform our lives. The root of love comes from God's divine gift of unearned and undeserved love for us. A natural out birth of love can then naturally flow from these roots and bear good fruit for God to share in this world, empowering us to truly love ourselves, love God, and love our neighbors.

It is by way of God's love for us that we receive the ability to know not just in our hearts but also in our minds and souls and spirits that we are deeply loved by a loving God, a God who knit us into creation and breathed life into us. We belong to God not by any merit of our own but by the simple love and mercy of God.

It sounds so simple, and yet it is one of the hardest practices of our lives. Allowing ourselves to truly receive God's love is intensely vulnerable. Brené Brown says "vulnerability is emotional exposure, risk and uncertainty." Allowing ourselves to receive God's love means knowing and owning deeply in our beings that we are loved by an incredibly gigantic, loving, and merciful God, and it means knowing that nothing can separate us from God's love. Nothing. We are not only loved, we belong just as we are, are loved just as we are. It moves me to tears every time I really meditate on this reality. As we receive God's love and begin to trust God's love, we are equipped to love ourselves, others, and God more fully.

I encounter people all the time who reflect a theology of deprivation and hustle, an active turning away from grace even if they aren't conscious of it. I watch so many around me act and believe just as I had my whole life. We live out of a deep and abiding belief that we have to earn our sense of worthiness and belonging. We feel we need to prove our worthiness for blessing and rest. And then we experience great fear at actually opening ourselves to the very blessing and rest we yearn for and have proven to ourselves that we have "earned." But the nature of God's love is that we cannot earn nor ever fully deserve God's love. The way we live our lives is so very counterintuitive to the definition of grace.

Opening to God's Love

Our relationship with God is a covenant, one in which we agree to show up and do life together. Yet over time, I've learned that it's frankly not as simple as choosing to engage or not engage, to open or stay closed off. As a spiritual companion, priest, and therapist, I've walked with many people who would love nothing more than to open their heart to a loving God and engage God from this open place. Yet something holds them back. Opening the heart isn't always as easy as sitting in prayer and meditation. Sometimes even asking the Holy Spirit to open our heart doesn't produce an open heart.

We may need to spend some time getting to know our heart better to understand why we stay closed off. Are we afraid of being hurt? Have we been hurt by God or by others in the past and we're fearful of being hurt again? Many find it helpful to connect with a spiritual companion, minister, close friend, or therapist to explore these questions.

I believe in a loving God that understands how hard life can be and how difficult it can be to trust. Many experiences in life warrant our wrestling with God. We can ask God the hard questions, such as "Where were you? Why did you let this happen? What does it mean that you love me in this situation?" It can be difficult to want to show up and open ourselves to a loving God when we don't even really know what that means to show up and open. I do believe our loving God adores our efforts, our intentions, our desires to connect even when it's hard, when it's risky, when it feels counterintuitive to what feels safe.

I believe God's loving us ("as I have loved you") is not a force; it's not a "have to"; it's not a push. Allowing God to love us and our ability to open to that love is a process that is easy and natural for some and hard and painful for others. Any of us can fall anywhere on that scale depending on what is going on in our lives. For some that have always found it easy to receive God's love, they can be uprooted and turned upside down by an event in life and not be able to open or connect with a loving God. For those who struggle with receiving God's love, a situation can break open their hearts in new ways that empower their ability to receive God's love in surprising and life-giving ways. There is so much mystery in both God's love and our ability to receive it. Let there be no shame if you struggle with receiving God's love. God sees you, hears you, appreciates whatever makes receiving arduous. God's love is in that too.

INVITATION TO PRACTICE: COMING HOME TO GOD WITHIN OUR SOUL

Sit quietly, allowing your body and mind to find some stillness, anchoring your attention in your breath. After a few moments of gentle breathing and settling into this time and space, place a hand over your heart. Allow yourself to breathe with your heart, the core of your being. Allow yourself to notice that God is here with you. The presence of God might feel far away, near, within you, or all of the above. Or you may not feel the presence of God at all. It's all okay. With your hand on your heart, simply allow yourself to be curious about the presence of God. Notice any genuine desire you might have to feel the love God has for you. Notice if you're open to feeling this love around you, near you, within you. You're not trying to will anything or make anything happen. You're simply noticing what is and allowing yourself to be open to experience even the smallest glimmer of God's love for you.

After a few moments of noticing, close your time with this prayer or one of your own.

Holy and gracious God, I pray that your Spirit might empower me to love you with all my mind, heart, and strength. May I have the courage to receive the love you offer so freely. May this love empower me to genuinely love myself so that I may love my neighbors from this deep inner well. Amen.

CHAPTER TWO

What Is Grace?

Grace is God's favor towards us, unearned and undeserved; by grace God forgives our sins, enlightens our minds, stirs our hearts, and strengthens our wills.

BOOK OF COMMON PRAYER, PAGE 858

An essential concept that is part of learning to love ourselves as God loves us is *grace*. We throw around the word "grace" in the Christian world—as well as the secular world—quite a bit. Even when used in a secular way (when people are not attributing a divine participation), *grace* conveys a sense of benevolence, perhaps even a tinge of something magical; something that cannot be fully explained. When grace is in action, it is as if both parties are giving to and receiving from each other with truly open hearts. When the word "grace" is invoked, something is happening that cannot be fully explained or understood, AND it's good.

The definition I not only use but also pray with is from The Episcopal Prayer Book, *The Book of Common Prayer*. In the back of this rather large book is a series of questions and answers, one of which is "What is grace?" The answer reads "Grace is God's favor towards us, unearned and undeserved; by grace God forgives our sins, enlightens our minds, stirs our hearts, and strengthens our wills." It's so easy to read this answer in almost a sing-songy kind of way and not take in the rich and abiding meaning that truly has the power to change our lives.

I've always changed the wording a little to allow for a deeper kind of resonance while maintaining the essence. Grace is God's love for us that we cannot earn nor ever fully deserve. This part about deserving used to really upset me. I thought it was a statement about humanity and our shamefulness. Over time, the Spirit has shifted my perspective on this. I now understand that through this grace, offered by a loving and generous God, God forgives all of the ways I stray and turn away from God's love, all the times I stumble and make mistakes. God respects and accepts God's own creation. Given our human nature and free will, we will stray; it's part of what it means to be human. Sometimes we may not even realize we are straying until we hit a bump that wakes us up.

By this grace, God opens my mind to receive the guidance of the Holy Spirit, offers me ideas I couldn't think of alone, and stirs my heart with love for myself and others as well as passion to use the power I do have for good. By this grace, God offers me strength and courage to carry out whatever God has given me to do to move forward the kingdom of God on earth.

Grace is meant to be lived with every breath of every day. Grace is meant to be received, understood, and embraced in every fiber and cell of our bodies. Grace is a reception and embodiment of God's love. Grace is a way of life because it is the cornerstone of our Christian faith. The essence of living a life of faith is receiving the deep and abiding blessing from God that we are God's beloved. Just as God said to Jesus in the Jordan River, "With you I am well pleased," grace is understanding that God says the same to each of us.

The Cornerstone Is Grace

If we seek to live out our faith in our daily lives, we'd be wise to consider what this looks like, what gets in our way, and how we might sustain this way of living with more ease. Given my journey with God, the cornerstone of my faith has become grace. Grace has become the lens through which I consider, breathe, and move in my faith, day in and day out. The journey to loving ourselves is about figuring out together what it means to come home to grace and live out of the deep and abiding love that God continues to pour into us.

What if we woke up every day and attempted, however imperfectly, to embody grace? Each day, I remind myself that grace is God's love for me that I cannot earn, nor will I ever be able to fully deserve it. And, by God's grace, God forgives all the ways I turn away from God's love and drift from the guidance of the Spirit. God's grace enlightens my mind, stirs my heart, and strengthens my will. I pray that I can be mindful each day of all the ways God's grace is manifest in my life. I pray for the courage to embody God's love for myself and others. And I pray that, by the grace of God, my humble efforts will make a difference in bringing forth God's kingdom.

As we breathe in each new day, we can envision ourselves moving through the day ahead with a calm and steady heart open to however God's grace may reveal itself during the day. We can even imagine our heart being stirred, our mind being enlightened to see things as God sees them, our will strengthened by God's courage to carry out what God has given us to do. When troubles and bumps occur (and they will), we can remember that by God's grace, we are forgiven for the ways we veer from God's will.

We also might imagine ourselves being agents of God's grace, so that as our hearts are stirred, our minds enlightened, and our wills strengthened, we are also open to the Holy Spirit breathing through us so that we may share with others the light of Christ, the breath of the Spirit, and the peace of God which surpasses all understanding. We are agents of God's love. We're called not only to receive God's love; we are also called to share it with others.

Claiming Our Belovedness

When we can truly receive and claim our belovedness from God, our lives are transformed. We become radically free to live and move and have our being in the Spirit. God moves in us more easily because our vessels are that much clearer and freer of debris. Claiming our belovedness is not selfish. True belovedness does not make us narcissistic; rather, owning our belovedness in God sets us in right relationship with God. It keeps God as God and us as humans not trying to compete with God for control. Claiming our belovedness shows reverence for God's design and creation.

Out of this deep and abiding blessing of belovedness, we are broken open to breathe. The movement of God, the breath of the Spirit is indeed breaking us open, freeing us from the binds and limitations of what holds us back in life. We live in a society that demands "holding it all together," which lends itself to perfectionism. But God calls us to accept our imperfections—and by doing so, we live more humbly in right relationship with God. What if, instead of trying to "fix" ourselves, we spent that time dwelling in closeness to God, one another, and our own souls? What if we used all our energy and resources not to portray the illusion of perfection, but to bless the world around us?

There is a blessing of balance here that we often miss entirely. As Christians, we have been notorious in our beliefs and actions that if we aren't serving others, we are useless, unworthy human beings. I find that women especially struggle with a sense of worthiness if they aren't serving those around them.

I believe when we take Divine love into our beings, it transforms our bodies, our hearts, our souls, our spirits, our very lives. Through this transformation, we are empowered with the capacity to truly, purely love our neighbors. God's love pours out of us and is offered to others. We become vessels of God's love.

So many people have shared that they cannot get to a sense of loving themselves alone. They need a sense of God's love for them first and a continued connection to that love. They need a well of love that they return to over and over again. The well is there, but we forget. We forget the well is there, and we forget to go back and be fed, nurtured, and nourished by it. We think we can love ourselves and love others on our own, but we do not generate that love all on our own. We don't brew our own love. We try, and we fail miserably. It's exhausting creating love on your own. And self-generated love is not the love of God. We must go to the Source of true belovedness to claim our belovedness for ourselves and to share that love with others.

This Divine love is the starting and returning place for all humanity. Divine love is home. We call it many things: Divine Love, God, Holy Spirit, Jesus, a Higher Power, a benevolent Force for Good, or simply Love itself. Whatever we call it, we must acknowledge something bigger, more benevolent, more kind than any individual in this world. The more we can accept and receive, really bring into our own beings this Higher, Bigger, Kinder Love, the easier it is to love ourselves and have genuine love to share with others.

Loving Ourselves: A Full-Body Experience

How can we learn to genuinely love ourselves? Loving ourselves can't only be a head exercise of learning about loving ourselves. It must be a full-body experience of loving our entire being. Loving ourselves as God loves us means taking in God's pure love and allowing it to transform our lives, including our capacity to love others by way of God's love flowing in and through us.

I often hear people talk about how lost we seem as human beings. We spend our days at work, catch some news, try to raise children as mindfully as we can, attempt to stay connected to the people we love most, follow politics, and remember with whom we're partnering in life. "Oh yeah! There is a loving God in the mix of all this!" Finding time these days to connect with our loving God feels practically impossible when competing with the very real, time sensitive demands of our daily lives. And yet when we take time for God to feed and nourish our souls, when we allow the Holy Spirit room to whisper into our minds and hearts, when we align the divine light within each of us with The Christ Light, it changes the very fabric of our lives. Every aspect of our day-to-day life can be transformed by God's love—every thought, every breath, every word, every interaction with ourselves and the people around us.

Right Relationship over Right Belief

God didn't send God's only son to earth to live among humanity simply to teach us "right belief"; Jesus came to teach us how to live in right relationship—in connection with God, ourselves, and one another. What I mean by "right" here is healthy, loving, kind relationships that are an outgrowth of God's love in us, relationships through which the Holy Spirit fills us with God's grace. In being filled, we receive the fruit of the Spirit *and* we offer the Spirit's fruit to ourselves and the world around us, the people we encounter, both strangers and those closest to our hearts.

We tend to create rules to provide a sense of safety and well-being for ourselves. In our vulnerability, we do this as humans: We create the illusion of control with rules and guidelines. Rules and guidelines are essential in a healthy life, as they assist in creating structure so that we can flow in the Holy Spirit and her guidance rather than being unruly and chaotic in the flow. However, when we become hyper-focused on the rules and structure, we can mistake them for God. We become so reliant on the rules and following the rules and ensuring others follow the rules that we forget the rules are simply there to create structure for the flow of God in our lives. The rules are not the point; they are not the destination. The rules point to the essence, which is connection with our loving God, ourselves, and one another. In creating all these rules, we attempt to become self-reliant rather than depending on God to guide us. We must learn or relearn how to lean on God for the sense of safety, wellbeing, peace, and belonging.

Managing Our Worthiness

We have become accustomed to managing our own sense of worthiness. This comes from a desire for control. We desire control more than anything. If we can earn something, then we can control it. If we can prove ourselves worthy through our good works and striving, we can control it. In doing this, we bend to a god of self-sufficiency and control. And this "god" keeps us hustling every single day, all day long. We have become slaves to our own hustle for control so much so that we cannot recognize our dance pattern. We cannot see that we spend our energy each day managing our own anxieties, fears, and desire for control, which makes it so much harder to call out and break the pattern. Our hustle becomes the fabric of our lives that we do not question.

Really looking grace in the eye calls out our hustle. Coming home to grace is about learning to be unbound to live our lives in the freedom of Christ to *live embodied grace*. True embodied grace requires moving the idea of grace from our heads to our hearts, to every fiber and cell of our being, and out through our hands, hearts, souls, spirits, and mouths. The theology of grace is about opening to God's love for us and allowing it to set us free. We are freed to live in the flow of the Holy Spirit. Freed to be transformed by God's love. Freed to share God's love with others. Freed to be unbound in our love for others.

Living Unbound

I have spent so much of my own life bound by the burial cloths of trauma and fear, peering out of the tomb of shame and anxiety. I want to step out of that tomb and be unbound to live the life God has given me to live. I see so many others around me with the same yearning, the deep desire to be unbound and start *living embodied grace*. When you've lived your life for so long bound by burial cloths, it can be really terrifying and mystifying to allow yourself to be unbound and live a radically different way, even when that way is infused and grounded in God's love.

We are people of habit and predictability. We like things to stay the same even if the same is not healthy and doesn't serve us.

We prefer the same, even if it keeps us bound and oppressed. On some unconscious or conscious level, we choose to not step out of the tomb into God's love and freedom. Therefore, we must have immense compassion for our habits and practices as we're simply trying to stay alive in this crazy world. Predictability is safe. It's easier to dance with the devil that you know than risk dancing with a potentially more dangerous and deadly devil.

Our brains and hearts often keep alternative options hidden. The option to stop dancing with this oppressive devil, to allow ourselves to be unbound by God's love, and to step out into the possibility of living embodied grace is scary because it is unknown. But we must recognize that we have a choice to make. We can keep the burial cloths intact, or we can open ourselves to the possibility of freedom and joy by way of grace.

Yes, God can set us free, but we have to be open and willing. We have to make conscientious choices to allow the burial cloths to unravel, to step out of the limited, confining tombs of our lives and into the voice of God calling us out into freedom. Naturally, there will be adjustments to the light from the darkness, the sense of freedom after being bound for so long, and the risks of living rather than staying stymied in sameness. Allowing God's love to penetrate our hearts, bless every fiber and cell of our beings, and transform our lives is a radical way to live. I believe God calls us to radical living. Each and every day, we can wake up and choose to *live embodied grace*.

INVITATION TO PRACTICE: ALLOWING OURSELVES TO BE LOVED BY A LOVING GOD

Sit quietly, allowing your body and mind to find some stillness, anchoring your attention in your breath. After a few moments of gentle breathing and settling into this time and space, you might want to place a hand over your heart. Allow yourself to breathe with your heart, the core of your being. Allow yourself to notice that God is here with you. The presence of God might feel far away, near, within you, or all of the above. Or you may not feel the presence of God at all. It's all okay. With your hand on your heart, simply allow yourself to be curious about the presence of God. Notice any genuine desire you might have to feel the love God has for you. Notice if you're open to feeling this love around you, near you, within you. You're not trying to will anything or make anything happen. You're simply noticing what is and allowing yourself to be open to experience even the smallest glimmer of God's love for you.

Notice feelings and sensations within your body associated with the presence of a loving God. Again, you're not forcing anything or willing anything to happen. You're simply making space for noticing "What is happening in my body when I pay attention to presence of God around me and within me? What is happening in my body as I attune to the very real love of God within me?" You may also notice any resistance you are feeling to noticing God's love. When we're not used to sensing God's love within and around us, it can feel really foreign and therefore uncomfortable and maybe even threatening to be with

God's love. Just notice. Be curious about what comes up for you to entertain the idea of opening to God's love.

When this meditation feels complete, you can close with this prayer or one of your own that resonates with you.

Holy and gracious God, I pray that I might drop all my efforts to earn and deserve your love. I pray that all the good I do in the world may flow from the love you wove within my being and continuously pour into me. I pray that you might forgive all the ways I drift from your love. Loving Spirit, enlighten my mind, stir my heart, and strengthen my will to yours so that I may be whole in you. Amen.

CHAPTER THREE

Receiving God's Favor Toward Us

Just as I have loved you, you also should love one another.
You shall love the Lord your God with all your heart,
and with all your soul, and with all your mind.
This is the greatest and first commandment.
And a second is like it:
You shall love your neighbor as yourself.

MATTHEW 22: 37-39

Several years ago, I was preaching at the morning chapel service at The Episcopal School of Knoxville about The Two Great Commandments that Jesus makes one. Jesus said to love the Lord your God with all your heart, mind, and spirit, and to love your neighbor as yourself. I asked the kids what Jesus meant when he said to love your neighbor as yourself. What did Jesus mean by "as yourself"? Did it mean I loved myself so much that I ate all my Halloween candy in one day because I wanted to? They were emphatic; "Noooooo" they came back to me. (As a mother, I was so pleased that they said no with such clarity and passion!)

"Is loving myself playing games on my mom's cell phone as long as I want?" They roared back at me, "Nooooooo." I was starting to get the feeling they thought I was a little nuts. So, I quietly said, "Well, what does it mean?" A few hands shot up, but mostly they sat quietly, many of them looking at me with a blank stare that mirrored my own questioning heart.

A quiet, thoughtful little girl in the third grade patiently was raising her hand, so I called on her. She very matter-of-factly said, "It's when we love us like Jesus loves us." My head tilted to the side. I took in her third-grade wisdom, allowing it to move from my head to my heart. Quietly, I echoed her words into the still chapel, "Right, it's when we love us like Jesus loves us." That's it! Who knows what I said after that. That little girl had preached the word of God and delivered the good news. I was simply there to set up the tee so she could swing.

As I drove away from school later that morning, I wondered to myself, "What would I have said if no one came up with anything?" To my surprise, I didn't have an answer. I wasn't sure what I would have said. I drove away noticing pangs of vulnerability in my chest; I needed to hear those third-grade words of wisdom more than anyone else in the chapel.

Loving God and Others: The Easy Part

For most of my life, "love your neighbor" has been the easy part. I have felt blessed with the ability to love and find the goodness in most people, including people for which it was harmful to me to find the good within them. In the three-part flow of love—God, others, self—loving others has been the easy part.

Loving God also comes easily to me. It feels instinctive, natural, and comforting to love God, as I have a deep and abiding sense that God loves me. The place where I always came up short was loving myself. In fact, many times I have thought, "I sure hope I love my neighbors way better than I love myself. Otherwise, my neighbors are in for it." I used to talk to myself in ways that I would never talk to even my worst enemy. I can have a tone that is nasty and downright cruel when turned on myself. My actions and inner thoughts betrayed my spoken theology of "Love the Lord my God with all my strength, and love my neighbors way better than I love myself." Sure, my lips would tell you otherwise, and my mind would believe every word I was uttering. But, deep down in my heart, I knew there was another truth—a truer truth, the truth that there was a big gap between my said theology and my lived theology.

Theology that Matters: Lived Theology

Our lived theology is what matters. The way we embody our faith matters greatly. In Matthew 6:21, Jesus tells us, "For where your treasure is, there your heart will be also." God knows us by the beliefs that guide our hearts on a daily basis, not so God can punish us but because God is trying to make God's joy complete in us (John 15:11). God wants us connected to the inherent God-given goodness within us and living from that place. God knows we're much more likely to suffer if we aren't.

My actions and inactions, my words and words left unsaid, my attitudes and way of being in the world—this is what my children pattern themselves after. How many times have I wished they were following my said beliefs rather than my lived beliefs? It's easy to utter good words; it's much, much more challenging to actually live by the words grafted in our hearts. *Wherever your treasure is, there your heart will be also.* God is bringing forth the kingdom of God not by our right utterances, but by our actions. What God and the world needs are our loving, kind actions. Our living grace is what God can use to transform the world and bring about the kingdom on earth.

Jesus shows us how to live in right relationship with God, one another, and ourselves. "Right relationship" is not so much about "right versus wrong." "Right relationship" is about living in connection to a loving God and to one another. "Right relationship" is allowing the breath of the Spirit to yoke us to the goodness with God and in one another. "Right relationship" is about staying right-sized with a loving God, remembering who I am in relationship with God and not getting my role mixed up with God's.

The Free Flow of God's Love

The essence of being in relationship with God is love. We must first receive it before we can authentically give it away. Otherwise, we're hustling love. We're offering the world love that we really would like back in some form or fashion. I'll love you and then you please love me back. We give so we can get. But God's love is meant to be a free flow of love. When we first receive the precious, nourishing, life-sustaining love of God, it changes our relationship to needing love back from others. People who are transformed by God's love and offer that love to the world are sustained by Divine Love and therefore don't cling to human love. They freely give without demand of love's return to them because God ultimately sustains their well of love. God created us for interdependency with other human beings, but not dependency. We need one another, and at the same time, we need to not depend on one another to provide the love out of which we love others.

The Awkwardness of Balance

One way I've noticed that I can detect whether I'm in hustle or flow is by noticing if I have any semblance of balance in my life. Balancing is never static; to truly physically balance, one has to constantly adjust and readjust. Balancing our priorities, activities, and values requires constant readjustment as well. I have a tendency to overextend myself.

Interestingly, we often feel expected to overextend ourselves in the name of faith. Somehow, we've absorbed the Protestant work ethic that if we're not always working, producing, caretaking, then we're unworthy of love and belonging. We worry we're not good Christians if we're not constantly serving. In particular, I hear this from other women: many have shared with me over the years that they feel like they have to be "fixing something" all the time. They feel a need and a responsibility to impose order and structure. They are a bit mystified to discover how difficult it is to let go and allow themselves to find a more centered and grounded relationship to the many tasks that make up their lives. I was mystified by this, myself.

On another morning, I led chapel at The Episcopal School, I asked a student to help me with an exercise in front of the student body. This student was an amazing basketball player. He had played with my younger son on a basketball team one spring, and it brought me almost as much joy to watch this child as it did my own. He had natural talent, and a joy for the game oozed out of him. I asked him to help, intending for his skill to help convey the message I wanted to share. I held a jar and he was to throw in marbles. As anticipated, he nailed every shot. What I hadn't planned for was that the marbles bounced off the bottom of the jar and flew back out. Whoops! This sweet, amazing athlete didn't know what to do. He wasn't sure how to get the marbles to stay in the jar—and I wasn't either. Just as I was thinking my children's sermon was a total bust, a kindergartner in the first row yelled out, "God does not need you to be perfect!"

My head shot up. I looked over to the front row to see who had uttered this gospel wisdom. A sweet little girl with passionate truth beaming from her face looked back at me. "God does not need you to be perfect." With that good news, I pivoted to a whole new sermon about how God doesn't need us to be perfect, whether that is making every shot or having everything perfectly worked out for every sermon.

Recently, I shared this story with a group of women. We all laughed at the little girl's boldness and wisdom. We shook our heads with the knowledge that we're often reminded of gospel truth from the mouth of babes. And we agreed that as much as we know she's right, we still don't know how to let go of striving for perfection. Just because we sense truth and wisdom deep in our bones doesn't mean we know how to let go and try a new approach. In fact, for many of us, even the idea of letting go of the hustle is terrifying. *If I'm not hustling, what then? If I'm not constantly serving, am I worthy of God's love?* So many of us order our lives, energy, and resources around relentless action—serving, work, and caretaking—that we have no idea what life might look or feel like if we pulled back on the throttle just a bit, much less if we shifted our lives into something that even remotely looked like balance.

So how do we do it—how do we start easing up on overextending ourselves and trust that a more balanced life of work and rest, action and inaction, serving and being served is okay? Can we trust that it's okay to seek balance, or do we still buy into the Protestant work ethic that the only way we're worthy of love and belonging is to hustle? Many of us need a permission slip that reads something like, "You don't have to hustle to be a good Christian" or "God needs you to rest just as much as you serve."

The even bigger challenge comes when we consider not only giving up a little of our serving, but also taking on the role of receiving. It's one thing to work on balance by not serving all the time, but it's a whole new thing to open ourselves up to receiving from God and others. I know that I'm infinitely more comfortable giving than I am receiving, and I know I'm not alone in this. When we're giving, we are in a position of power and agency. We get to decide what to give, how much to give, when to give, under what circumstances to give. Even when our giving feels overwhelming and compulsory, we are still in the driver's seat. We also feel the rewards, the pleasure and delight in offering something to someone else.

Learning from How Mary Received and Changed the World

We can learn about the balance of serving and receiving from Jesus' mother, Mary. Mary receives the blessing and favor of God, and it literally changed the world. The angel Gabriel and Mary dance with each other. There is this flow of conversation that is energetic, a giving and receiving of God's love. Mary receives the blessing and favor, and also she gives of herself by saying yes.

In the Gospel of Luke, the angel Gabriel comes to Mary and says immediately, "Greetings, favored one! The Lord is with you" (1:28). Mary is unsure how to receive this greeting. Her instinct is confusion, doubt, and fear. On some level, she must be thinking, *I'm just this young girl about to get married. There is nothing in my life that indicates a sense of worthiness for blessing or favor. You have the wrong Mary.* Because she is such an unlikely candidate for favor based on societal norms, maybe on some level Gabriel's words feel like a set-up or a trick.

Gabriel responds to her fear and doubt. "Do not be afraid, Mary, for you have found favor with God" (v. 30). Then the angel goes on to tell her about this son she will give birth to. Hearing all this, Mary goes to logistics. She asks how she can possibly have a baby, much less one that will save the world, when she hasn't even had sex. Here we see the Holy Spirit play a role unlike any other in scripture. Gabriel says, "The Holy Spirit will come upon you, and the power of the Most High will overshadow you" (v. 35). I understand this to say the Holy Spirit will fill up Mary and offer the power of God to make all things possible through her.

In addition, Gabriel shares the good news about Mary's cousin Elizabeth, who even in her old age will give birth as well. Gabriel summarizes these holy occurrences by saying, "For nothing will be impossible with God" (v. 37). The immediate recognition is that God is making the impossible possible through Elizabeth—it will clearly take a miracle for her to bear a child in her late age. But Gabriel's statement also hints at the impossible that God will birth through the vessel of a teenage girl.

When Mary hears Gabriel's words that nothing is impossible with God, I imagine clarity opens within her heart. If nothing is impossible with God, then maybe she can fall within the realm of favor and blessing. With this assurance that all things are possible with God, Mary steps into God's call on her life. She says,

"Here am I, the servant of the Lord; let it be with me according to your word" (v. 38). She doesn't start negotiating with the divine messenger; she fully surrenders to God's will.

Affirmation of God's Favor

Humbly, Mary takes on the spiritual cloak of favor. According to the Gospel of Luke, she sets out to visit her cousin Elizabeth. I imagine all the days of walking gave her a chance to meditate on and embody being favored—we know now that bilateral movement offers the brain a chance to integrate experiences and process understanding in healthy and meaningful ways. It is as if each step gave her a chance to integrate her encounter with Gabriel throughout her mind and body, so much so that by the time she arrives on her cousin's doorstep, she has become a fully embodied vessel of God's favor. Elizabeth and the child within her womb immediately recognize the blessing within and upon Mary. Elizabeth is filled with the Holy Spirit and, from this filled-up place, cries in a loud voice (as if the Spirit is speaking right through her vocal chords), "Blessed are you among women, and blessed is the fruit of your womb. And why has this happened to me, that the mother of my Lord comes to me? For as soon as I heard the sound of your greeting, the child in my womb leaped for joy. And blessed is she who believed of what was spoken to her by the Lord" (v. 42-45).

Elizabeth's declaration of blessing for both Mary and her baby must have been an overwhelming affirmation for Mary. Having a spiritual encounter can be isolating, and it can be easy to begin to wonder, *Did that really happen?* The logical mind can quickly discount the breath of the Spirit in our lives, the intuitions and nudges, the blessings and favor. To have her beloved cousin filled with the Holy Spirit upon her greeting and offer insight into what had transpired with Gabriel must have been heartening. If I were in Mary's shoes, I may have thought to myself, *Oh! This is really happening!*

Elizabeth shows her own humility when she asks, "Why has this happened to me, that the mother of my Lord comes to me?" Elizabeth acknowledges the honor and privilege simply to be in Mary's presence and the presence of the child she bears. Spiritual encounters are often terrifying in nature, because we have no idea what is truly being asked of us but sense something of great magnitude. It makes sense that we become nervous if not terrified with a spiritual encounter. Yet Elizabeth's response conveys a message of joy—whatever this blessing is upon her young cousin, it brings joy to the child in her womb, and Elizabeth allows that joy to flow out of her. We can feel Elizabeth's excitement and awe as she greets Mary.

It is the last part Elizabeth says that moves me every time I read it. "And blessed is she who believed that there would be a fulfillment of what was spoken to her by the Lord." Over and over, Mary's active role is acknowledged and praised. It would have been easy for Mary to have declined Gabriel's request, telling herself she wasn't worthy of the favor and blessing. It would have been easy for Mary to move on after the encounter with Gabriel and act as if it had never occurred. I wonder if Mary hadn't accepted the invitation, would the Holy Spirit have found another woman to bear the Christ Child into the world?

But Mary stepped into the call on her life. "Here am I, the servant of the Lord; let it be with me according to your word." Elizabeth's words affirm that Mary made a choice. Mary leaned into embodying grace. And in choosing to step into the call on her life and believing there would be a fulfillment of what was spoken to her by the Lord, Mary set the wheels in motion to carry forth God's kingdom on earth. If Mary had found herself unworthy of the call, if she had determined she was not up to the task, if she had refused to receive the blessings of God, we would be in a very different story right now.

In response to her encounters with Gabriel and Elizabeth, Mary is able to genuinely speak aloud "My soul magnifies the Lord, and my spirit rejoices in God my Savior, for he has looked with favor on the lowly state of his servant" (v. 46-48). She is speaking aloud what flows from her heart. Right there, Mary names her lowliness. She owns that she is far from royalty or from anyone in society who would be thought worthy of favor. When reading this scripture aloud in a Bible study, a friend of mine declared, "Well, that is a woman who owns her worthiness in God!" We too are called to own our worthiness in God and accept the favor God extends toward us. How might it change our lives to embrace God's favor toward us? In little ways or big ways, how might it change the world?

Let's be mindful that "change the world" can feel daunting and unrealistic. We forget that simply allowing ourselves to be loved by God and receiving God's favor inherent in that love is transformative in and of itself. Receiving God's love and favor does change the world one soul at a time. Imagine if everyone around the world were open and received the love of a loving God and claimed the God-given favor within that blessing. What a game changer that would be! While we are powerless over what and how other people live their lives, we do have the agency to work with our own heart, our own lives, our own connection to a loving God. This intentional act and way of being has the power to change the world.

Breathing with *Nothing Is Impossible with God*

The key in my own practice of living grace is that I have to believe in my worthiness of favor so that I can fully open to receiving that favor. I must lean into God's love and trust that I am worthy of that love and the blessings that love pours upon my life. I cannot cut off favor and blessings by a lack of faith in my own worthiness. Sometimes believing in my own worthiness feels like too much of an ask. So I've learned to lean into the Holy Spirit and ask her for help. I pray for the Spirit to clear out what blocks my ability to open myself to favor. I ask the Spirit to connect me with the worthiness that God wove within my being. I pray for the Spirit to open my heart to teach me about my inherent worthiness and how we are all created for God's favor.

INVITATION TO PRACTICE: RECEIVING GOD'S GRACE

Sit quietly, allowing your body and mind to find some stillness, anchoring your attention in your breath. After a few moments of gentle breathing and settling into this time and space, place a hand over your heart. Allow yourself to be curious about the presence of God. Notice any genuine desire you might have to feel the love God has for you. Notice if you're open to feeling this love around you, near you, within you. On your inbreath, allow yourself to receive the love of God, even if only momentarily. On the outbreath, allow that love to settle into your being.

Repeat to yourself, "For nothing is impossible with God." You can say the first part of the phrase as you breathe in and the second part as you breathe out, breaking where it feels natural for you. Allow these words to become a prayer for your life. Notice the feelings and sensations in your body as you take in these holy words that weren't only true for Mary and Elizabeth, they are true for all humanity for all time. "For nothing is impossible with God."

When this practice feels complete, end with this prayer or with one of your own.

Holy and gracious God, may your Spirit open my heart so that I may fully come home to your love that already exists within me. When I struggle to feel your love or even waver in fully believing in it, may your Spirit bring me home to the deepest truth and wisdom within me, which is your love. Amen.

CHAPTER FOUR

Wrestling with "Unearned" and "Undeserved"

When he came to his senses he said, 'How many of my father's hired hands have bread enough and to spare, but here I am dying of hunger! I will get up and go to my father, and I will say to him, "Father, I have sinned against heaven and before you; I am no longer worthy to be called your son; treat me like one of your hired hands."' So he set off and went to his father. But while he was still far off, his father saw him and was filled with compassion; he ran and put his arms around him and kissed him.

Luke 15:17-20

But she came and knelt before him, saying, "Lord, help me." He answered, "It is not fair to take the children's food and throw it to the dogs." She said, "Yes, Lord, yet even the dogs eat the crumbs that fall from their masters' table."

Matthew 15:25-27

I have struggled all my life with the idea of receiving God's love into my own being, coming home to myself in the love of God. Maybe I've struggled with this because I'm a woman. Many women in our culture struggle with feeling worthy of love and belonging—though a lot of men struggle with this too. Maybe it's because I grew up in the south. Historically, ideas of southern hospitality and culture don't cultivate much opportunity for a woman to feel worthy of love and belonging, given that the understood focus is to be on "others." That is why it is often so much easier for southern women to love their neighbor rather than love themselves. We presume it's an all or nothing proposition. We either love others or love ourselves. Yet, God calls us to love our neighbors as we love ourselves—both are essential. As I worked through childhood trauma in therapy, I have learned to acknowledge the specific things within my past that led me to feel bad about myself. I subconsciously internalized that I was bad because bad things happened to me, and my deep need and desire to be identified as good felt illusive.

So much of my own healing has come from healing my sense of unworthiness. I've explored the spaces where my spoken theology and lived theology do not align. I've challenged what I really believe about the loving God I say I believe in. I've questioned what I believe regarding how God made me, made all of us, and what that means for how I see, speak to, and treat myself and others. For me, it's taken a village to wade through these waters—spiritual directors, therapists, mentors, dear friends, and family members.

Most of us have experiences in life that leave us feeling bad about ourselves. Shame kicks in the stress responses of fight, flight, freeze, fawn. The feeling that we're not worthy of love and belonging can take us to our knees. So the hustle to make good grades, stay out of trouble, be a certain weight and size, maintain all relationships with ease and perfection can all be genuine goals and also can represent a deep desire to avoid feeling shame for not measuring up.

Shame in small doses is a healthy emotion. It's absolutely needed to keep us in check as social creatures moving through life together. Many of us consciously or subconsciously supersize shame, however, and it becomes problematic in our bodies, our minds, our hearts, our souls, our relationships, and our lives.

Shame tells us we don't measure up. But grace indirectly tells us that we can't measure up—the very nature of grace as unearned and undeserved means that we cannot earn it and we cannot create a way to deserve it. Much of what prevents us from being able to live fully from a place of grace is the disconnect between these two realities. We are surrounded by messages demanding that we earn and prove worthiness at every turn. But God asks us to accept the gift of grace that requires nothing for it to be offered. Yet *unearned* and *undeserved* are baked into the bread of a life of faith, part of the fabric of our existence with a loving God.

The interaction of shame and grace create such a place of irony. The key is to hold this disconnect loosely. It is difficult to hold "earning" and "deserving" loosely when we live in a culture that demands we earn and craft a sense of deserving in order to be found worthy. At the same time, we can easily assume that because we cannot earn or deserve grace, God finds us lacking and disappointing. This definition could work against our self-esteem and our ability to love ourselves. How are we simultaneously favored while also undeserving? How can we be both favored in the eyes of God while also undeserving of God's grace?

It seems counterintuitive to make a case for favor and then jump to claiming that grace cannot be earned nor deserved. We so often connect the earning/deserving dots to lead to the belief that we are undeserving, which then provides a quick exit to shame. But when we shift the puzzle pieces around, a different picture emerges. Grace can neither be earned nor fully deserved because that is the nature of God, not us. Grace is a gift from God that holds almighty power to transform our lives. Saying grace is unearned and undeserved is a statement about how abundant, generous, and almighty God is, rather than a statement about how unworthy and undeserving we are.

Time and again, the scriptures illuminate how we as humans deem ourselves unworthy and undeserving, while our loving and generous God works to reframe our understanding of his love. There are multiple stories in the Bible that have helped me wrestle with this seeming dichotomy between favor and undeserving: Mary being approached by the angel Gabriel, the woman threatened with being stoned, Levi the tax collector, just to name a few. But the one that has helped me the most is that of the prodigal son.

Look Again for God's Grace Circle

The prodigal son (Luke 15:11-32) is a story rich in unearned and undeserved grace. The parable guides the hearer from a human perception of love to a divine understanding of love. Jesus even tells the parable because he overhears the Pharisees grumbling about the love he is showing tax collectors and sinners. While their words simply state the facts of who Jesus is spending time with, the undertone of their conversation carries bitterness, anger, resentment, and judgment. The Pharisees have drawn a human circle of grace; they have decided who is in (themselves) and who is out (sinners and tax collectors). They find it maddening that Jesus is not respecting their understood delineation of grace. Jesus' behavior threatens their world order and their self-justification of their behavior.

In response, Jesus shares this parable of a man with two sons. We first get to know the nature of the younger son who seems to have dreams running wild in his eyes. He asks his father to divide up the inheritance now rather than waiting until the father dies. Surprisingly, the father agrees and does so. The younger son, likely always looking for a good time, sets off with his share in his pocket to presumably greener pastures and bluer skies.

He quickly squanders the money and finds himself living in poverty amidst a famine. He hires himself out and takes a job feeding pigs in a pasture. One day he wakes up to see his reality for what it is. He contrasts his situation with the situation of his father's hired hands. The people who work for his father always have something to eat. In fact, they always have something to spare. So the son decides to go back to his father and ask to work as one of his hired hands, deeming himself unworthy to ever be called a son again.

As he travels home, his father sees him from a distance. Upon seeing his son, the father is filled with compassion. He runs to him, grabs him in a hug, squeezes him for dear life, and kisses him.

The son has readied himself for this moment. Even though his father is lavishing him with swiftness, embracing and kissing, the son says the words he has practiced. He owns his own demise. He says, "Father, I have sinned against heaven and before you; I am no longer worthy to be called your son." The son draws himself outside the circle of grace. Rather than play into the son's perception, though, the father sets into motion a celebration. He dresses his son with a fine robe and ring and calls for the best food to be prepared for the evening's festivities. Who knows what the understanding will be in terms of the finances of the situation. The father makes clear that what matters most is acknowledging the son's belovedness.

"This son of mine was dead and is alive again" (v. 24). The father didn't know if he would ever see his son again, and now this son has returned to his warm embrace. Though the son has deemed himself undeserving of his father's kinship, the father's love brings the son home to the foundation of their relationship, which is love. No matter the son's transgressions, there is no behavior that can separate him from the love of his father. So though the son perceived his behavior to move him outside the circle of grace, his father's love quickly reminds him that there is nothing that can keep him from his father's love and favor. Nothing.

Let us not forget that this father had another son. Upon the return of the younger son, the older son begins to act like a true eldest child. (I speak as an eldest child myself.) He clearly doesn't even know his brother is home because he asks a servant what all the commotion is about. Unlike his father, he has not been anxiously waiting for the return of his younger brother. The servant tells him that his brother has returned and there is a party underway. You may take note that the brother doesn't run to his younger brother and embrace him and give him a kiss like his father did. In fact, he doesn't move a muscle. He stands right where he is, and it seems his heart hardens with bitterness rather than opening with compassion.

The father comes out to speak with him. He is likely encouraging him to come enjoy the party. Welcome your brother home! Instead, however, the older son digs in his heals and gives words to his resentment. All this time, he has been loyal to his father. He has done everything "right." He has followed every last rule and has exceeded every expectation. And yet the father has never thrown even the smallest soiree for him and his friends. The father responds to his resentment by saying, "'Son, you are always with me, and all that is mine is yours. But we had to celebrate and rejoice, because this brother of yours was dead and has come to life; he was lost and has been found'" (v. 31-32).

The older brother makes a case for earning his father's love and being deserving of celebration. He argues that his steadfast loyalty and following of all the rules is what makes him deserving of favor and love. The older brother has deemed himself worthy and deserving of being within the circle of grace, and he resents that his younger brother has squandered his inheritance and deemed himself unworthy and yet still finds himself dancing within the circle of grace. As an oldest child, I understand the older brother's perspective—I would feel bamboozled by the whole situation. It's very hard to give up the human-made grace circles we've created when we've been hustling our whole lives to ensure we've "earned" our way into the circle.

This parable reminds us that as humans we really like to have control or at least the illusion of control. We want to have some say in our ability to have access to grace, and we want other people to earn their grace as well. The younger brother deems himself unworthy before the father can beat him to the punch and deem him unworthy. I have spent most of my life finding fault with myself faster than anyone else can because the sting is just ever so slightly easier if (like the younger son) I've rehearsed what it sounds and feels like to be found unworthy and made the call myself. The older son, on the other hand, dots every "I" and crosses every "T," ensuring that no one can find fault with him. Anyone looking at the report card of his life would have to agree he is worthy and deserving of his father's love; his actions have earned him the right to fall within the circle of grace. Like the older brother, I have hustled to make sure I'm found worthy. So many of us find ourselves in this double dance of being terribly hard on ourselves earning our way in and berating ourselves when we fall short.

And oh, how real the hustle is when we engage God's love this way, working both sides to make sure we're always covered. We find fault with ourselves before anyone else can, while simultaneously hustling so that ten-out-of-ten people will be sure to find us worthy of grace. If you work both sides, you're always covered, right?

Except when we work either side or both, we're missing grace completely. Attempting to earn love flies in the face of true grace. We cannot earn it. And beating ourselves up for every mistake or potentially perceived mistake also means we're not living grace. The essence of grace is that God takes deserving and earning off the table. Worthiness is not up for grabs. We continue to crave the illusion of control because it makes us feel safe in a crazy world. But the foundation of grace comes from an abundant and generous God who isn't concerned about our human delineations of worthiness, deserving, and earning.

Potential Shame Trap

Not being able to earn God's grace nor ever fully deserving it was a shame trap for me. I deeply wanted to earn God's grace because I wanted to control it. I wanted to ensure my reception. If I couldn't earn it, it felt like I was leaving it up to chance, and that wasn't comforting. That left my sense of trust wobbly. If I could hustle and create the illusion of assurance of grace, I felt much more comfortable, even safe and secure. But what this revealed was that I was not trusting God to deliver. In fact, by trying to earn God's grace, I was undermining the covenant with

God. I was swimming in God's lane rather than staying humbled in my own. I can't earn grace. No one can.

God's love isn't about what we can do for God. Grace isn't about our worthiness as much as it is about God's abundance. We can sigh in relief—God's love isn't up to us. It's unfathomable in this world where everything appears to be purchased, bartered, negotiated, and leveraged. Everything comes at a price. It's no wonder that we have such a hard time grasping the abundance of God's love. It's no wonder we struggle mightily to simply receive without trying to earn our way.

In addition to receiving grace on God's terms (not ours), we're also called as Christians to respect the circle of grace God has drawn for all of humanity. All of humanity—all of creation—belongs within the circle of grace. Though we may want to deem certain people as unworthy of belonging, God shows us time and time again that everyone belongs within the circle of grace.

Grace challenges us not only to receive God's love but also to share that love with others. We must refrain from outcasting ourselves from grace. This can be a spiritual discipline, the work of actively not hustling for grace while also refraining from the temptation to treat others as if they do not belong within the circle of grace either. Truly living into the essence of grace helps us grow ever closer into the nearness of God and empowers us with the ability to love our neighbors as ourselves.

The bestower, the granter of grace, is not our human mind, behaviors, words, or perceptions. The granter of grace is God, in the role played by the parent in the parable. There are several instances within this parable that highlight the benevolence, kindness, and generosity of God. The one that grabs my attention is how the father sees the younger son while he is still far off. It is as if the father has been watching for him, waiting for his return, maybe even anticipating his return. His attentiveness toward his son allows him to notice when the son appears even while still far off.

A Loving God Always Waiting for Our Return

The image of the father waiting anxiously for his son's return resonates with the loving God I have come to know in meditation. God is always waiting for my return, anticipating my arrival back into God's loving arms. The awareness of this loving God who is always awaiting our return has changed how I experience my own wandering mind and my life through the experience of meditation. Sure, my mind wanders. It's a mind doing what a mind does. When I notice that my mind wanders, I use it as an opportunity to intentionally bring my mind back to the anchor of my body and/or breath. I don't have to judge myself for having a busy mind or berate myself for sucking at meditation. Rather, I can joyfully anticipate being welcomed home yet again by a loving God upon my return home to my body and breath. And there are days that being welcomed home again and again is what I need far more than keeping my mind as still as my body.

Like my judgmental mind, it would be reasonable to expect that the father might be filled with anger, resentment, and bitterness seeing his son coming back empty-handed and desolate. Yet this father is filled with compassion upon seeing his son. Rather than being angry about the suffering his son has brought upon him, he is moved with love and concern.

I believe this is the Holy Spirit filling the father up with gifts of the Spirit. The breath of the Spirit can take many forms when we are filled by that movement. In this case, the stirring of God within the father creates an opening to be filled with compassion. Compassion is understood to be the turning toward suffering: *com* meaning *with*, and *passion* meaning *suffering*. To be with someone in their suffering is the essence of compassion. And there is no greater teacher of turning toward suffering with love, kindness, and empathy than Jesus.

When we are filled by God's compassion, we are empowered with an ability to turn toward our own suffering and the suffering of others that would normally be too much for us to witness. As human beings, we are often affected by the pain and suffering of others, and it can be difficult to truly see someone in pain, especially someone we love like our own child. And yet that is exactly what we are called to do—part of our inherent life together on this earth is learning, by the grace of God, filled with God's compassion, to turn toward the suffering of others with love, kindness, and empathy.

Our human instinct is to turn away from our own pain and the pain of others. Therefore, it takes the filling of the Spirit to empower us to do what we need to do, what we're called to do, and frankly what others need us to do. If we are to create safe spaces of love and belonging with one another, we have to be willing to see one another in our pain, our darkness and suffering, and bring the fruits of the Spirit with us into those liminal spaces.

I wrote this prayer based off another prayer that has been so very meaningful to me for years:

> The extremities of this wild world we live in call for
> everything to be held in love.
> So may our hearts beat with the love of God within us
> that nourishes every fiber and cell within our being.
> May our eyes behold all of God's creation as sacrament-
> an outward sign of the very real inner grace.
> May our hands touch in ways that reveal Jesus' love in
> the washing of the feet.
> May our lips speak all truth embedded in the love God
> has woven within us.
> May our souls be so lit with the brilliance of God that
> it transforms our lives and is a beacon of hope for
> those around us. Amen.

The father in this parable is the embodiment of "May our hands touch in ways that reveal Jesus' love in the washing of the feet." It's as if the father cannot stand to be away from his son for one more second! After months, perhaps years of not seeing his son, not knowing where he is or if he'll ever see him again, with the chance to reunite, he runs to close the gap as quickly as possible. He embraces him in a way that conveys far more than words—"You are the beloved." Every child yearns to be delighted in by their parents. It is to the benefit of all children to see their parents' eyes light up upon seeing them.

Compassion is a way of being rather than particular words we use. I imagine that the twinkle in this father's eyes could light up a city. The father had no need to say, "Son, I have such compassion for you." The son would have known it instantaneously by the look in his eye, the quickness of his steps, the warmth of his embrace. It was the Spirit that filled the father with compassion. The father merely became a willing vessel of God's love and kindness. The father was open and willing to embody grace and share that grace with his son.

Even Crumbs Are Enough

How do we claim the truth that we are undeserving of God's love yet maintain a sense of worthiness? For those of us who have wrestled the demon of shame most of our lives, this component of undeserved grace is a potential nightmare. There is a woman in the Bible who took me on a journey to wrestle with God over this shame.

She appears in the Gospel of Matthew, in chapter 15, verses 21-28. I love this woman who approaches Jesus. She is shouting at him, clamoring to get his attention. "Have mercy on me, Lord, Son of David; my daughter is tormented by a demon." The scriptures say, "He did not answer her at all." Jesus is flat out ignoring this woman. And the disciples want her gone as well. She is annoying them with her screaming. She's demanding way too much attention.

Jesus draws a circle around his ministry in this moment: the sheep of Israel are in and everyone else is out. He so clearly defines his purpose right here—"I was sent *only* to the lost sheep of the house of Israel." Boom! Just like that, he cuts this woman and her daughter off from his healing.

This woman is humbled in her desperation to save her daughter. She is so afraid. When life throws us into darkness, we get really clear about what true light looks like. She knows Jesus is her answer; she knows he can save her daughter. Jesus is the Light for which she's been looking. So, she does what any mother would do: she doesn't take no for an answer.

Humbled, kneeling at his feet she utters these words: "Lord, help me."

Jesus' response is so unlike the Jesus we know and hold in our minds and hearts. "It is not fair to take the children's food and throw it to the dogs."

Even being aligned with a *dog*, this mother doesn't back down. She comes right back to him, "Yes, Lord, yet even the dogs eat the crumbs that fall from their masters' table."

Silence.

I can imagine Jesus saying to himself, "What did she just say?" *Yes, Lord, yet even the dogs eat the crumbs that fall from their masters' table.*

This woman in her terrifying darkness, seeing the potential to lose her daughter to this demon, knows in her bones that even a crumb of light intended for a mere dog would be enough to heal her daughter.

Can't you just see Jesus' face soften as he tilts his head to really look at this woman? Now he sees her; he really sees her. He sees the pain and desperation and terror in her eyes. And he sees her heart, her faith. He knows she is putting her trust in him. He can see the truth resonating from her soul through her eyes—he is the Light she's been looking for.

This passage follows another discourse where Jesus is trying to explain what defiles. "What comes out of the mouth proceeds from the heart" (v. 18). What comes from this woman's heart is pure faith in his ability to heal her daughter. The people surrounding him, including his disciples, still struggle to understand the fullness of who he is—maybe even Jesus himself is struggling to understand. They can't quite capture the essence of his message that relationship with God, others, and self are about love and mercy. It's not about what we eat and don't eat or whether we wash our hands or not. It's not about following a list of rules. Faith is about what is in our hearts. It's about the words that pour from our mouths, that flow from our hearts. Faith is about God's love that emanates from our being. If our hearts are pure in knowing, being in relationship with our loving God, trusting the movement of the Holy Spirit in our lives, then pure words pour from our mouths and build up others and ourselves.

I love the woman's persistence. I love how Jesus shifts his perception. I love that a woman helps him see through a different lens. I love that in this one little interaction, the circle Jesus has drawn around himself and his ministry widens. Jesus becomes the Messiah and healer for *all* people. There are no exceptions. God's love and mercy knows no bounds; it extends to everyone.

And all it takes is a crumb, just a tiny crumb left under the table for the dogs.

What I find so fascinating about this woman is that she is so bold in her sense of worthiness. She is so confident in her worthiness that she is content aligning herself with the Messiah's categorization of dogs. This woman has within her a deep and abiding sense of worthiness already, so much so that she is capable of not backing down from Jesus. She senses deep in her bones that the crumbs under the table meant for the least of these is enough to save her daughter. How bold and benevolent and powerful is the healing grace of God.

I wonder what made this woman so bold. I wonder what gave her the tenacity to not back down. Maybe it was her abiding love for her daughter. Maybe it was that primitive drive within a parent to protect and save at all costs. Maybe it was being in the presence of the true Light. Maybe she was a vessel of the Holy Spirit reminding Jesus of the fullness of his call to and with all of humanity. Maybe the energy flowing between this woman and Jesus enlightened Jesus' heart to be the Messiah of all people, to draw a circle of grace that included everyone.

It is such a humbling story in the Gospel of Matthew where even Jesus appears to be getting it wrong at first. It appears his grace isn't for everyone. He understands he has come to save his people, the Israelites, and get them back on track with their God. This woman's soul has the power to see this man as a Savior not only for the Israelites but for all people, which includes her and her daughter. She boldly draws herself into the circle of grace. She captures Jesus' attention by saying even the dogs are being blessed by gathering up the scraps of grace underneath the table. If the dogs are worthy, aren't all people outside the flock worthy of the holy crumbs?

Grace is so extravagant that even God's crumbs are holy. God's scraps are sparkling lights underneath the table. Rather than taking the language of unworthy and undeserving as yet another opportunity to beat ourselves up with shame, it's an opportunity to see God as abundant. God doesn't need our hustle. In fact, our hustle distracts us from living the lives we're called by God to live. There is a big difference between living each day trying to earn our sense of worthiness with God, ourselves, and one another, and starting each day trusting we are already worthy.

Embodying grace is about getting up in the morning and grounding ourselves in a sense of the love God has already woven inside us and continually pours in and through us moment by moment. We then become free to live our lives in the flow of the Holy Spirit doing the next right thing guided by the Spirit. Grace is a game changer for how we live our lives day in and day out. No more of this hustling for worthiness. No more trying to accumulate data points of deserving. No more hammering away a need to earn, earn, earn love and belonging. Allowing ourselves to receive God's grace, to truly take in God's love and allow it to transform our lives, changes everything.

Embodying Grace within Healthy Boundaries

Though all people belong within the circle of God's grace and we are to extend grace to others, it is important to be discerning of how close to be with people who have hurt us and the people we love. You can extend grace to people *and* keep them at a distance. This is called having healthy boundaries. Boundaries are utilized to protect our needs, not to punish other people. We get to decide what our needs are and how best to protect them. Sometimes we are made to believe that being a "good Christian" means we can't have any needs or that we must fully embrace people who have caused us harm. This is horrible theology. We can forgive others and still maintain healthy boundaries with them. If people aren't going to change their harmful behaviors, attitudes, and/or words, then they aren't safe to be around. Our loving God yearns for our wholeness and healing. We cannot live into our God-given wholeness and healing and allow people's toxicity to invade our lives. Wisdom is called for in discerning how close to be with people, especially those who have caused harm and trauma. We can allow others to live within the circle of God's grace and yet not live within our sphere of influence.

The story of the prodigal son is really about the parent who embodies grace; the parent who loves no matter what. God is the Father of this parable. Remaining humble means we allow God to be God, and we remain human. We don't try to drift into God's lane, grabbing for control, either by being in charge of who receives grace or in charge of delivering that grace to every person. We allow God to be the parent who embodies grace. We get to be the mere mortals that we are who can embody and extend grace and also stay in our wholeness by protecting ourselves with healthy boundaries.

INVITATION TO PRACTICE: ALLOWING YOURSELF TO WRESTLE WITH GRACE

Sit quietly, allowing your body and mind to find some stillness, anchoring your attention in your breath. After a few moments settling into this space, place a hand over your heart. Allow yourself to breathe with your heart, the core of your being. Notice that God is here with you, and be curious about God's presence. Notice any genuine desire you might have to feel the love God has for you. Notice if you're open to feeling this love around you, near you, within you. Be curious about what, if anything, closes you off or blocks you from receiving God's love and favor toward you. Notice feelings and sensations that arise in your body as you notice any blocks. If you start to feel overwhelmed or stressed by the awareness of your blocks, slow your breathing down. Use these words as you breathe in: "I receive God's love." Breathe out without any words and notice any feelings and sensations of love settling in your being. Allow this rhythm of breathing to be a gentle witness to your blocks and the feelings and sensations, emotions you have about your blocks. Keep your breathing slow and calm. When you're ready to conclude this practice, close with this prayer or with one of your own.

Holy and gracious God, help me be aware of the ways I block myself from receiving your grace. May you heal the wounds within me that create angst over receiving your grace fully and wholeheartedly. May I learn to turn toward my own suffering with the heart of Jesus so that my suffering is relieved in your love. Amen.

CHAPTER FIVE

Living Grace in Our Bodies

Do you not know that your body is a temple
of the Holy Spirit within you,
which you have from God?

1 Corinthians 6:19

Our Bodies: A Gift of Grace

What would it be like to wake up every morning with the assurance that our bodies are precious and perfect as they are—temples of the Holy Spirit? One of the hurdles of living an embodied faith is actually getting into our bodies, owning our bodies, being kind to our bodies, and listening to our bodies for wisdom and guidance from the Spirit.

We live in a culture that is obsessed with the perfection of bodies. We photoshop the lines, wrinkles, weight, shape, and color of almost every photo before sharing. We don't even need professionals to help us with this anymore. We have smartphones that give us the ability to edit. We are constantly bombarded by images of "perfect" people that inform how we should look and what we're striving for. I have spent far more time in this precious life thinking about some aspect of perfecting my body rather than listening to the wisdom of my body. By the grace of God and a lot of work, that mindset has shifted.

Treating my body as part of the gift of grace has become a spiritual discipline. I had to stop demanding perfection from my body and instead lean into kindness and love for this vessel God gave me. I want to care for my body because it is a chapel of the Holy Spirit. When I began to turn away from cultural perfection standards and turn toward the reality that this body is a vessel of the Holy Spirit, it shifted how I care for this vessel. Over time, I realized that I wanted to eat more kale not because some magazine told me kale would give me killer legs but because it was one of the only foods around that actually made me feel good.

I have always loved walking, and over the years, I realized how beneficial exercise is to stabilizing my mood, sugar levels, and energy. I also discovered that bilateral movement like walking, biking, and swimming helps clear the cobwebs from my mind. I can see situations in my life more clearly when I move my body. Part of this realization blossomed into the beautiful awareness that as I cleared the cobwebs from my mind and muscles, I was coming home to the love of God with more ease. It's as if I was also clearing the cobwebs of the spiritual vessel of my being which cleared the way to arrive at home once again with my loving God. The Holy Spirit can more easily reach me and breathe through me when I care for my vessel. When I take the time to clear the pathways for the Spirit's breath, I can align more easily with the breath of God.

Another aspect of living an embodied faith is learning to use tools that allow us to listen for the wisdom of the body. Again, there is so much buildup that happens over the days, weeks, months, and years of our everyday lives. It's as if our vessels become clogged and tarnished by the wear and tear of daily life. This isn't a bad thing. It is just part of the natural way of life. Our vessels create buildup. We have to learn ways to sweep, brush up, or even scrub, when necessary, our vessels to make room for the breath of the Holy Spirit to breathe in and through us. Even when our vessels are cleared and all channels are open, it still takes intention to be still and listen for the wisdom to bubble up. We learn to attune to the wisdom and be patient for it to arise. All of this takes some intention, patience, and practice.

Learning to trust that our body is our friend and on our side is part of the work. For so long, even within the Christian faith, we have been taught not to trust our bodies. We believe our "flesh" will lead to sin, fire, and damnation, and we downplay any importance of the physical for fear of it leading us further from God. It's rare for a church to talk about the beauty, strength, and usefulness of the body and how the body is part of the grace God has given us, rather than something that is always working against grace.

We don't learn that following the Holy Spirit requires listening and trusting our body to offer wisdom and guidance. We're not taught that our bodies are good and part of God's grace. If we're not given permission to listen to our bodies, we will not find the wisdom that the Spirit has woven there.

Though our bodies can be part of our turning away from God (like our minds, hearts, souls, and spirits can as well), we've gone too far when it comes to vilifying the flesh. Our bodies are one of our greatest gifts given to us while we walk the earth. Our body is part of how we live and move and have our being (Acts 17:28); the body takes in life-giving air and unifies our breath with the breath of the Spirit. Our bodies help us move through the world. They hold babies and loved ones. They kiss and hold hands. They make love. They see words in books and breathtaking landscapes. They taste food that sometimes seems straight from heaven. They hear music that enlivens the soul and brings tears to the eyes. Our bodies can bring us so much joy. It would be a completely different experience here on earth if we were merely souls drifting about without a body to shelter and temple the divine light within us.

Missing the Wisdom of the Body

Certainly, the Enlightenment further severed the natural connections between mind and body. We became a people who prized the intellect and mind and further labeled and condemned the body. Our human tendency to split and categorize things as good and bad became stronger during this period of history. It could be argued, however, that Christianity split mind and body shortly after Jesus ascended to heaven. The Gospel of Mary shares a narrative that portrays Jesus as someone who didn't see the body as bad or problematic. And quite possibly Mary helped Jesus' ministry in holding this wisdom to the Light.

When the gospels were canonized and Mary's Gospel along with others were left out of the official Bible, the wisdom of the body fell aside. The Christian faith has been wandering in the desert for a long time, wrestling with this tension between mind, body, spirit, and soul. Yet it is the Spirit herself that is guiding us back to the wisdom that these parts that make up our whole being are not meant to be in tension with one another; rather, we are called to align with the Spirit, which creates alignment within our body, mind, spirit, soul. It's as if the Holy Spirit breathes right through us and pulls a thin, light string so that our body, mind, spirit, and soul not only align with one another but also orient to her. In this alignment, we can best hear the wisdom of our bodies and follow the flow of the Spirit.

So many bodies that have walked this earth have been abused, beaten, taken advantage of, scorned, brutalized, and shamed. It's no wonder that we turn away from our bodies completely. When the body holds recent or long-ago trauma, it can be difficult to turn toward and befriend the body. So many people survive trauma because they momentarily or for long periods of time separate from their body. It is a tremendous gift God wove within our bodies to be able to not feel or be in our bodies at all times. What can be problematic over time, however, is that the body returns to separating even when it doesn't need to for survival. The mind may perceive danger, become fearful, and then automatically separate body and mind to create a sense of safety.

Stress in Our Bodies

Given the heightened amount of stress people report to be experiencing individually and collectively around the world, it seems most of us are having heightened stress reactivity in our everyday lives. When we experience stress, our mind calculates that whatever we're encountering is more than our inner resources can manage, hence a stress response. Sometimes what we're encountering is an external situation—the loss of a job or a loved one, the end of a relationship, a shortage of food, difficulty paying the bills, trouble with a coworker. Sometimes the stress we're encountering is internal—we feel fearful, depressed, anxious, with our minds spinning a million miles an hour. Many of us experience chronic sleeplessness because of our heightened stress response as well. When we cannot regulate our nervous systems during the day, it makes it very difficult to sleep at night.

Stress is often a combination of external situations that compound our internal reactivity to whatever we are experiencing. For example, rather than calmly coping with a fender bender, we instinctively begin to beat ourselves up, chastising our lack of attention or carelessness, or we start raging at the other driver, focusing our stress response on them and blowing up the situation by a hundred-fold. Whether external cues or internal cues or a combination of the two, the perceived lack of ability and resources to manage the situation causes a stress response. The research has shown we don't experience stress within our thinking brains only, we experience stress within our emotional brains and within our physical bodies as well. Stress gets lodged in our bodies. It gets stuck in the very place our Christian faith has taught us to separate from. To truly heal and move forward and to engage our resiliency, we must engage our bodies. By the grace of God, the light of Christ, and the breath of the Spirit, we must learn to turn toward our bodies, our God-given vessels, and to merge and work with them rather than against them.

For those of us who have experienced trauma, working with a mental health professional can be exceedingly helpful in working to reconnect with our bodies. Trauma happens in relationship, and we heal in healthy relationship. Many of us need a nurturing, knowledgeable guide to assist this work so we don't get overwhelmed in the process of reconnection. The appendix has further resources that can assist your journey.

Along with therapy, the spiritual discipline of meditation has given me a way to come home to my body. It offers a way to practice noticing the feelings and sensations in my body in a way that feels safe and inviting. One of the most beautiful parts of weaving meditation with Christian faith is that, as Christians, we do not take the journey home to our own bodies alone. The breath of the Spirit is directing us home. The Light of Christ is the lighthouse calling us and lighting the way home. The love and peace of God which surpasses all understanding is both accompanying the journey home as well as patiently awaiting our arrival. We are surrounded by God's love and the Trinity at work in and around us, guiding and accompanying us, awaiting our arrival while also enjoying the journey.

In my own recovery from childhood trauma as well as years and years of repeated stress overload, I found that turning toward my body was terrifying at first. Though intuitively I knew my body could be trusted and was oftentimes befriending me even through very unpleasant feelings and sensations, stress had taught me to fear my body. We are wired to retaliate from pain. Our human instinct is to turn away from physical, emotional, mental, or spiritual pain. Part of the discipline is learning to trust God and ourselves so much so that we can override that instinct to turn away and allow ourselves and God to be with that which is painful.

It is in our turning away, in our freezing, in our fighting, and in our fleeing that so much suffering occurs. Taking the hand of God and turning toward our own pain is one of the hardest things we may ever do, and yet we can with God's help. We are fully equipped by the grace of God to be with that which is painful inside us. Not only does this strengthen our ability to connect with ourselves and God, it builds our ability to trust ourselves and God as well. In addition, the more we strengthen this ability to be with pain and suffering within ourselves, the more equipped we are to naturally (from a place of inner God-given, well-honed strength) be there for others in their times of pain and suffering as well. God uses the strength we hone within ourselves to share the grace of God with others when they need it most.

Maybe listening for the wisdom of the body comes easily for some people. In some aspects, it came intuitively to me, and in other ways, listening for the wisdom of my body was as difficult as learning a foreign language.

The Deception of Body Perfection

I grieve how much time I have spent consumed with the appearance of my body. As a child, I danced five to six days a week from the age of nine to sixteen. There was a heavy emphasis on our weight and the shape of our bodies. It was common for someone to get picked on and shamed in front of the entire company for her weight. I share this story because it shows how normal it is to indoctrinate girls in our society with the demand of perfect bodies. And when we don't measure up, shame ensues. The reality is that most girls don't need a dance teacher criticizing her body in front of twenty-five other girls to learn to be mean to herself about her weight and size. From movies and television, social media, and advertisements, girls learn quickly what is expected of their bodies. Dance teachers, parents, siblings, teachers, friends, and coaches oftentimes merely amplify the constant recording playing on the inside. *Be perfect. Be perfect. Be perfect.* It is not only girls—raising sons has enlightened me as to how much bodily perfection is now also geared toward boys and men. There seems to be a war in the public sphere against our bodies, no matter our age or gender.

With all this subconscious and even conscious messaging, it's easy to start believing that we are worthy of love and belonging only if we are a certain size and shape. Our worthiness hinges on our ability to literally fit into a certain size pair of jeans. Suddenly, it doesn't matter that God's love is unearned and undeserved. We're so busy holding ourselves accountable to society's standards of physical perfection that we completely lose sight of the fact that God's love is not dependent on our size. We might not love ourselves regardless of our waist measurement, but God surely does. Do we care that God's love is not dependent on our physical size? Does grace matter when how we spend our time and energy every day shows that our treasure is a body shape? I know I spend too much of my time and energy on my body shape, but is that what I want to reflect my treasure? Can I love myself regardless of my body shape and size?

We should not become gluttonous beings because our shape doesn't matter to God and really doesn't need to matter so much to ourselves. The difference of intention is what matters: if I'm going to start treating my body like the gift of grace that it is, a vessel of the Holy Spirit, then I have to make healthy choices about getting enough movement and eating nutritious meals to fuel this beautiful body. I have to be intentional about drinking enough water and getting enough sleep. What's interesting is that my days pre-living grace and now attempting to embody a living grace likely look very similar to the outsider. I still try to exercise four to five times a week. I still try to make conscientious decisions about what I put into my body. And I still spend a good deal of time shooting for optimum sleep. Nothing has changed so much with my behaviors, but what drives my behavior has shifted radically. My purpose for healthy behaviors is not to reach some milestone of perfection, but to care for the body I have been given. It's no longer about loving myself or finding myself worthy of others loving me only if I'm a particular size. What drives these behaviors these days is an acceptance of the body God gave me and an intention to care for this vessel so that it functions as well as possible. When I care for my body, it tends to literally and figuratively move with more ease in the flow of the Spirit.

Sacraments are an outward sign of an inner grace. We can view our bodies as sacraments and can understand our physical activity and healthy eating as outward signs of God's grace working within us. Our bodies are truly a gift from God that can and will remind us daily that we are God's beloved, gifted with unearned and undeserved grace. It is through our bodies that we experience God's forgiveness of our mistakes, enlightening of our minds, stirring of our hearts, and strengthening of our will.

For example, we need our actual bodies to register when our heart is being stirred. It takes paying attention to sensations and feelings within ourselves to notice, "Oh, my heart is so stirred over this!" Without these feelings and sensations, it's really hard to know when God has sent the Advocate, the Holy Spirit, to stir up passion within us. Think of a time when you had a sense of knowing, a curiosity, or a gentle nudge of the Spirit. You may want to close your eyes to make your awareness more focused. Notice feelings and sensations in your body that register this knowing. When my heart is stirred, I feel both a slight excitement in my chest with also a deep peace that runs through my chest at the same time.

Divinity Wrapped in Skin

It's not an accident that God decided to take human form, to have flesh, feelings, and sensations. We needed a Messiah with flesh; someone we could relate to, whose actual actions, words, and energy we can live by. As human beings, we are powerfully interconnected by energy, brain state, and emotion. It's hard to figure out how to love the Lord your God with all your heart, mind, and spirit without a role model, someone you can see and hear and touch. We clearly needed God with flesh to help us understand how not only to live in covenant with God but also how to live in covenant with ourselves and one another.

Jesus continues to be made manifest in the world. God grafted his Son like he has grafted humanity for eternity. His divinity is wrapped with cells, nerves, organs, and the beautiful, largest organ of skin. Jesus used not only his words but his actions and inactions to teach us how to live an embodied grace. He showed us what it looks like to have your heart stirred (John 11:17-36), your mind enlightened (Matt. 15:21-28), your will strengthened (Matt. 4:1-11; 26:36-46). He showed us what it looks like to do something with that God-given wisdom.

For years, I've been captivated by the story of Jesus in his resurrection appearing to the disciples in the upper room (John 20:19-23). On his first appearance, everyone is there except Thomas. Later, when they tell Thomas about their encounter with the resurrected Jesus, he doesn't believe them. He says to the disciples, "Unless I see the mark of the nails in his hands and put my finger in the mark of the nails and my hand in his side, I will not believe" (v. 25). Thomas is so very clear about what it's going to take for him to believe. He's asking for an encounter with Jesus, and maybe more importantly with Jesus' body. Thomas needs to be able to use his human senses (in this case touch) to actualize belief. He doesn't just want to hear Jesus' voice or see him with his eyes. He says he needs to actually touch the very places on Jesus' body that are indications of his hanging on the cross. He wants to go straight to the source of Jesus' death if he is ever going to believe in his resurrection.

What captivates me is that upon Jesus' resurrection, God did not return Jesus' body to "normal." God is God. If God can bring Jesus back from the dead, God could most certainly fully heal Jesus' hands and sides. It's curious to me that a fully resurrected Jesus is a Jesus with wounds. Over the years, I've come to believe this is not an accident.

Upon Jesus' second appearance (John 20:26-29), he speaks directly to Thomas: "Put your finger here and see my hands. Reach out your hand and put it in my side. Do not doubt but believe." The eyes of Thomas' heart are opened; he sees and knows Jesus for who he is. He exclaims, "My Lord and my God!"

Jesus knew what Thomas needed to believe. Over the months of ministry together, walking alongside one another, Jesus got to know Thomas, got to know how his mind and heart worked. It's really kind and empathic that upon his second appearance to the disciples, he says "peace" to everyone and then directs his comments to Thomas in a way that would speak directly to the heart and mind of Thomas. Again, this is Jesus meeting someone right where they are. Jesus also calls Thomas on what he needs. He says, "Have you believed because you have seen me? Blessed are those who have not seen and yet have come to believe."

Jesus is both meeting Thomas where he is, giving him the very evidence he needs, while also calling him into a deeper, more abiding faith, a faith that doesn't require quite so much evidence. Because what is faith, after all, if every last bit of it is right before our eyes, at our fingertips, and ringing in our ears? I also think Jesus offered this challenge not only to Thomas but to all those who would come to hear this story. Jesus knew most disciples would not have the luxury of seeing, hearing, and touching him.

The most important part of this story for me is that it was Jesus' wounded body that provided the evidence for Thomas' belief. If Jesus' hands and side had been left with no indication of the nails and spear, would Thomas have been able to believe? What does it say about our theology that we follow a Messiah with fully healed wounds that still show evidence of injury?

In our culture, we rarely expect full healing to include evidence of the wounds. We don't believe we are fully healed if there are any remaining indications of previous injury on our body or in our heart, mind, soul, or spirit. These notions separate us from our loving God. "I'm too broken to be healed." "God surely cannot love me with all these inner and outer wounds." "Surely I'm not worthy of love with all these piercings to my soul." It is difficult to love ourselves, much less our neighbors, when we carry around our inner and outer wounds and assign them narratives that separate us from the love of God.

Jesus' own miraculously resurrected body holds evidence of humanity's attempt to break him. This truth speaks to how God might see us and the evidence of our brokenness. Perhaps living resurrected lives ourselves means owning our wounds and imperfections as part of the narrative written in and on our bodies. Perhaps how we embody our wounds becomes part of our faith.

Perhaps our wounds and imperfections are the very thing that draw us into deeper connection and unity with a loving God and with one another.

Jesus' wounds tell the story of how he overcame death on the cross and lived into the resurrection and ascension. His wounds become the very place where Thomas believes. His imperfections (by society's standards) are integrated and become part of the salvific narrative of his life. God saved Jesus not by removing the pain and suffering of human cruelty and death itself, but by offering him new life through the pain and suffering of life.

We experience injury and death throughout our lifetime. Deaths occur when life doesn't go the way we want it to or plan for it to or think it should go. Deaths can happen when we have to let go of the way we think life should be going and accept reality on reality's terms. Life is constant change, and all change includes some form of death; the death of what we once had or expected to have, even as something new is birthed in its place. We are hardwired to resist the pain and suffering inherent in experiencing death and loss. Yet the question becomes what is God doing through this loss? God does not create or cause the loss. Life happens; losses happen; part of life is experiencing the losses. But God uses these life circumstances to bring us closer. Our wounds lead us to experience eternal life on earth. If we embrace the love of God in the midst of our loss, we find that God is actually working through our loss to set us free. Our wounds that reflect our loss become the very things that lead us home to grace, to an embodiment of deep inner peace.

INVITATION TO PRACTICE: BLESSING OF YOUR BODY

Allow your body and mind to find some stillness. Anchor your attention in your breath. Be curious about the presence of God's love with you. Then do a simple body scan, anchoring your attention in each part of your body:

Feet—remember that God loves your feet just as they are.
Legs—remember that God loves your legs just as they are.
Hips—remember that God loves your hips just as they are.
Stomach—remember that God loves your stomach just as it is.
Back—remember that God love your back just as it is.
Chest—remember that God loves your chest just as it is.
Lungs—remember that God loves your lungs just as they are.
Heart—remember that God loves your heart just as it is.
Shoulders—remember that God loves your shoulders just as they are.
Throat—remember that God loves your throat just as it is.
Face—remember that God loves your face just as it is.
Mind—remember that God loves your mind just as it is.

Now notice feelings and sensations throughout your whole body. How does it feel to see and experience God's love through your whole body? What are you noticing?

End your body scan with this prayer or with one of your own.

Holy and gracious God, thank you for loving me just as I am. Thank you for helping me see my body just as it is and loving it as you do just as it is. May your Spirit continue to breathe in and through me and keep me grounded in your love that flows through me eternally. Amen.

CHAPTER SIX

Embodying Grace Mindfully

Mary took a pound of costly perfume made of pure nard, anointed Jesus' feet, and wiped them with her hair. The house was filled with the fragrance of the perfume.

John 12:3

Kneeling: Choosing Where to Place Your Embodied Attention

Mary, the sister of Martha and Lazarus, is notoriously kneeling at the feet of Jesus. All these years, I've loved all three of these stories of Kneeling Mary, and I've missed how they weave together. When you stitch together the stories of her from the various Gospels, you find a woman who must have known Jesus incredibly well. We see that Mary had a practice of kneeling at the feet of Jesus, allowing her heart to be stirred and sharing her stirred heart with Jesus. Through her practice of kneeling with Jesus, she became part of God's further illumination of the Messiah and teaching the embodiment of God's love. Her interactions with Jesus help us understand how we might embody grace mindfully and allow our hearts to be stirred, empowered to be part of God's unfolding goodness in this world.

Though we don't know a lot about the women in the Bible, we have the privilege of getting to know this Mary, sibling to Martha and resurrected Lazarus, through her multiple interactions with Jesus. This Mary is pivotal in helping to illustrate at least three stories in the life and ministry of Jesus.

One of those stories is the well-known Mary and Martha story (Luke 10:38-42). Martha is fit to be tied because Jesus has come to visit, and her sister, Mary, is just sitting there at his feet, listening to him talk, for crying out loud. Martha seeks Jesus' help by asking him to ask her sister to get up and help. Lunch isn't just going to appear on the table all by itself. Jesus tells Martha, and I imagine it stings more than a little bit, "Martha, Martha, you are worried and distracted by many things. . . . Mary has chosen the better part." We might hear it as "Martha, Martha, you aren't embodying grace mindfully. Your sister is choosing to embody grace mindfully. Join her."

For years, I never stopped to wonder what exactly Jesus was telling Mary while she knelt at his feet. I never stopped to consider what content Martha was missing as she bustled about the kitchen. I've always been so guilt stricken by how I act like Martha, I'd never considered the wisdom Jesus told Mary while she knelt. It never occurred to me that perhaps Jesus was telling Mary that one day he was going to need her to do something daring and bold—he would need her to anoint his body while he was still alive, walking, talking, and embodying the good news. What if Jesus was asking Mary for her help? He needed her to carry out God's plan by helping him get the attention of those around him. He needed her action of anointing to shock the disciples into the reality that he was going to die sooner rather than later. He needed the anointing to point to the inner grace woven within him. Jesus didn't need to be reminded of his inner grace. The anointing was a wakeup call to the inner grace within humanity, within every single beating heart, every soul being breathed into by a loving God. He needed them to wake up and pay attention to what he was sharing with them while he was still among them in body and soul. She would need to use the remainder of the expensive perfume to anoint his body for burial after his death. What was transpiring at the feet of Jesus was wisdom, truth, love, and divine kingdom goodness.

If Mary had been preoccupied with the to-do list of the day as was her sister, she likely would have missed the invitation to be part of carrying out God's plan. Whether Jesus actually articulated the ask of Mary or not, as Mary sat at Jesus' feet listening to whatever he shared with her, I do believe her willingness to embody grace mindfully opened her heart to be stirred by Jesus. What transpired between them was the illumination of God's grace. Their heart connection, the flow of God's love between them, was an outward sign of the inner grace woven deeply between them. And this love was putting into motion the call on Jesus' life, that which he was called to embody in this world, so that we might have some clarity as to how to do the same. Mary's action of sitting at Jesus' feet was a model for how we might act in this world, how we might live into the work of listening to Jesus, how we might receive the love of God and allow it to empower us to be the love of God in the world. Through sitting at Jesus' feet, we are equipped and empowered to do hard things when called upon by a loving God so that God's goodness might spread through this wild and complex world.

The Intimacy of Sharing a Broken Heart

There is another dynamic encounter between Jesus and this Mary in John 11. When Lazarus dies, Martha speaks to Jesus first and then goes to Mary and says, "The Teacher is here and is calling for you" (v. 28). Mary quickly gets up and goes out to Jesus. She kneels at his feet and says to him, "Lord, if you had been here, my brother would not have died" (v. 32). Mary shares her broken heart with tears streaming down her face. Jesus is deeply moved by Mary's weeping and all those who are weeping for Lazarus as well. He is so moved that Jesus himself begins to weep. Like the father in the parable of the prodigal son who is moved to compassion when he sees his younger son from afar, Jesus is filled with compassion, moved to tears because the people he has been carrying around in his head and heart are in pain. Mary's heart was stirred with grief over the loss of her brother, and Jesus' heart was stirred with Mary's grief. This is so true of all of us social creatures, isn't it? We are so often moved by what stirs other people's hearts.

In this story, Jesus encounters a grieving community. He is simultaneously attuning to Mary's heart while also engaging the broken hearts of all those weeping around her. It is curious how the flow of love between Mary, Jesus, and the members of the village may have impacted Jesus' next decisions and words. It's so easy to think of Jesus as simply doing his Jesus thing without being impacted by the people around him.

My whole life I've imagined Jesus going through pre-set motions of God's call on his life, carrying out the kingdom work God gave him to do. It's only been in recent years that I have begun to wonder how Jesus embodied the new mandate to love one another as God has loved us. Yes, Jesus' words are truth and life, and the way he lived his life is embodiment of God's love. The flow that love created between him and others is what makes his life and ministry transformative. The more I read the Gospels and allow the Spirit to stir my heart, the more curious I become about how Jesus himself embodied "love your neighbors as yourself." I'm fascinated by how Jesus was living his new mandate to "love one another as God has loved him."

Jesus is the embodiment, the ultimate example for Christians, of loving others *as yourself*. Jesus is infused with the love of God. Every fiber and cell of his human and divine body, soul, and spirit breathes with the Spirit, and his heart pulses with the love of God. This breath of the Spirit and vibration of God's love is his true ministry on earth. He shows us what we're not only capable of as human beings, but what we're called to live as Christians. Living the love of God in our own cells, our own hearts and minds, and sharing that love with others is the good news. Jesus embodies the gifts of the Spirit in his being, actions, words, and attitude. Love, joy, peace, patience, generosity, kindness, gentleness, faithfulness, and equanimity are the essence of his being. His way of being in his own skin and in the world illuminates our own essence. His way of being in the world is our way of being in the world. It doesn't mean it's easy! The Way may be simple, but it isn't easy. If it were easy, we wouldn't have needed such a captivating example in Christ. If it was within an easy grasp, humanity wouldn't have resisted his embodied wisdom with such deadly force.

Empowered to Act with a Stirred Heart in the Face of Anger and Confusion

In the very next chapter following Jesus' encounter with the community grieving Lazarus, we find this same Mary kneeling at the feet of Jesus (12:1-8). This time, however, she is kneeling before Jesus in a private gathering of men. I've always been moved by the story of this daring woman willing to touch Jesus and anoint him with costly perfume. It would have been odd for a woman to be present for a conversation of an inner circle of men. And it would have been completely unheard of for a woman to touch a man outside her family. Mary has kneeled at Jesus' feet, listening to him speak, despite her sister's protests. She had kneeled with tears streaming down her face after her brother's death. Once again, Mary kneels at Jesus' feet, this time doing something far more intimate and bold than simply listening or speaking. While he is still alive, she anoints his body. She wipes his feet with her hair. During the time that she has sat at his feet and listened and through her openness and vulnerability to share her life and pain with her beloved friend and teacher, she has truly seen Jesus the Messiah for who he truly is. She has allowed herself to be empowered by her connection to Jesus. She is willing to act in ways that will be ridiculed and make people angry.

All four Gospels recount a story of a woman anointing Jesus with oil. Only John names this woman as Mary. Matthew and Mark have Jesus say at the conclusion of the event that any time this story is spoken of, it will be shared "in remembrance of her" (Matt. 26:13; Mark 14:9). This loyal woman was bold enough to anoint him in the face of angry and confused disciples. Just as Mary has anointed Jesus, his words give credence to her courageous heart and anoint her as the prophetess she is. His words are an outward sign of an inner God-given grace, her open heart and strength to act in the face of anger and confusion.

Mary is an amazing example of how our connection to Jesus and God matters. How we own our relationship with God and how we draw near to Jesus as Mary did sets the course of our daily lives. If we make room to kneel at his feet in meditation, in prayer and study, in friendship and worship, we are far more likely to hear from our loving God. We're far more likely to tap into the wisdom and courage as Mary did. We're far more likely to have our hearts stirred in the nearness of God. We are better able to live from the inherent goodness of God that is already within us.

A Heart Song to God

What I see and hear in the life of Mary, this woman who knelt at Jesus' feet and listened, who openly wept and shared her pain with him, who bravely anointed him even though it angered those around her, is a woman who loved the Lord her God with all her heart, mind, soul, and spirit. Mary's actions are nothing short of a heart song to God and the beloved Son. Mary's willingness to draw near to Jesus, to be informed by his wisdom, and to be transformed by his embodied love emboldened her to be an agent of God's love and joy. She too became an embodiment of God's love.

When we stitch together the stories of our lives, does a heart song emerge? Do the stories of our lives add up to a life well lived drawing near to God, singing a song of love to God? Do the stories of our lives show us loving the Lord our God with all our hearts, minds, souls, and spirits? Does that embodiment empower us to love ourselves and one another well?

Be Still and Know that I am God

Years ago now, I set off for my first five-night silent retreat in New England. I really wasn't sure what to expect. Were we really going to sit in silence for five days together? Would people try to cheat? Talk in the bathrooms? Would I want to cheat? I was delighted and terrified at the idea of handing over my cell phone for five days. How would I make it without my cell phone for five whole days? As I took my seat among the roughly thirty participants, I could sense I wasn't the only one with some jumpy nerves. Everyone else looked more than a little curious about what we had signed up for.

The facilitator put me somewhat at ease that first day. She had a kind face and a strong yet gentle voice. I could tell this was not her first rodeo. We were in experienced hands. And sure enough, we were invited to put our cell phones in a basket and would get them back upon leaving.

As I moved through the days and nights, I found the hardest part was having to sit with the parts of my life that weren't working and caused me so much anxiety. I had nowhere to go, nowhere to run, nowhere to hide. I couldn't start checking my phone. I couldn't distract myself with the busyness of my everyday schedule. I couldn't even read a book to take my mind elsewhere. They even encouraged us knitters not to knit. I quickly noticed how I wanted to use food to numb the discomfort I was in. Though not a coffee drinker, I have never delighted more in the coffee they roasted right there at the center. It was an unexpected love note from God in liquid form; really it was a vehicle for the comfort of cream and sugar.

The only words I uttered aloud that week were in a twenty-minute one-on-one check-in with the facilitator. The gift she offered in those swift twenty minutes was normalizing the fire of my mind, my anxiety, the difficulty I experienced in sitting with what was troubling me. Instead of running, hiding, distracting, numbing, I was being given the rare opportunity to sit and stay with my experience and breathe through it. I was encouraged to allow the discomfort and pain to move through me rather than get stuck and lodged within my body and mind. I learned how to allow it simply to be—not fix it, minimize it, or blow it up, but to let it be.

After that brief interlude of speaking, I resumed silence through the days and nights, enjoying each outdoor walk, yoga pose, and pain in my spine as I sat in silence for prolonged periods of time. Before we all flew away from this intense, silent experience, we got to share with one another anything we'd learned or experienced, any takeaway from the week. What I shared was that I had come hoping to find two things: shortcuts to coming home to myself and a greater ability to stay home with myself once I got there. My experience that week taught me that there are no shortcuts, and staying home is a discipline in and of itself.

The irony, however, is that over the years the more I practice breathing through rather than getting stuck, the more shortcuts appear. The more I surrender to the path of going home to my own soul by way of paying attention to the feelings and sensations in my body, the greater capacity I seem to have in staying home.

When I flew home that night, my husband, Andy, wanted to hear all about my experience. What was it like being silent that long? Did I get restless? Was the food good? Did everyone abide by the invitation to be quiet? Ever the verbal processor, I didn't have too many words. I felt a bit like I was floating through my home that first night back. My body was trying to integrate the experience of sustained silence with being back in my normal, loud world. My sweet husband said to me that night, "You have learned more about mindfulness in these five days than I have learned reading about it for the past ten years." I could feel the resonance of that truth.

What I couldn't talk about at the end of the retreat, having been in a secular setting, was that in learning to come home to myself, I discovered I was also coming home to a loving God within me. Five days and four nights of "tush on the cush" kept showing me that I *never* sit alone. Even when my mind was on red hot fire or anxiety was coursing through my veins, if I could get still and stay still, I would eventually realize God was right there with me. I was never arriving home to an empty house. There was a loving presence waiting with ease, kindness, and compassion. It was such a vulnerable and tender realization. Coming home to the divine every time proves to be just this for me—vulnerable and tender.

Coming Home to a Loving God Who Resides Within

Some might say that I was learning to come home to the kind and gentle presence of my own being. I'm sure that is partly true. Yet there is a distinct feeling of presence that is more than just little old me. More than a human presence. More than a part of myself. It is hard to put into words, so maybe at this time I can still only say, it felt and continues to feel like coming home to a loving God. Over time, I've felt the desire to grow this experience of coming home to a loving God. This desire motivates me to get my "tush on the cush" in regular fashion, both to calm my nervous system; check in with my own being in mind, body, soul, spirit, and heart; and connect with a loving God.

As I have shared this with people, sometimes someone asks if I can always feel that presence of a loving God with me in meditation. I cannot. I don't always feel the presence, and yet, there is some sense of presence even when I cannot feel it. Maybe sometimes it feels more like trusting the presence is there even when I cannot feel it. It brings me home to the essence of God's wish for humanity through Jesus—Emmanuel, God with us. Meditation offers me the opportunity at any moment of my day to simply come home to the reality that God is right there with me, and I imagine I will spend the rest of my life grateful for this.

Being with Darkness

People shy away from meditation and mindfulness—really any form of getting quiet and looking inward—because it can be a daunting task. Meditation often involves sitting with parts of ourselves that the church has long made us feel bad about: any inner darkness, sin, or mistakes. For hundreds of years, the church has spoken of (really, been obsessed with) original sin. The hyper-focus on sinfulness has not only shamed people, but it has also created relentless trauma that remains for generations. It is one of the leading reasons people are turning away from church.

As people of a loving God, do we miss the mark? All the time! But our loving God does not want our mistakes flaunted about in our face all the time. Shame makes us reactive and fearful. It wreaks havoc on our self-esteem and on our relationships.

The Jesus I read about in the Gospels does not shame people for their sin. God is interested in where we veer from God's love, where we miss the mark, where we distance ourselves from love in order to bring us back to that love. But more often than not, we have turned our missing of the mark from a method to gauge how we are living in union with God into a weapon we use to judge and punish. Shame becomes a way to control.

Slowing ourselves down through mindfulness and meditation can restore us to connecting with our essence, which is whole and holy. We can breathe with the Spirit and allow ourselves to be breathed by her. We can remember that we are God's children and remember that God yearns to live in closeness with us. We can embody the very aspects of our essence and become vessels of the fruit of the Holy Spirit for others.

As I have sat in meditation, I have found that in the stillness, moment by moment, I kept coming home to God within me. Of course, there are many moments where my mind is drifting to the worries, fears, and concerns of my life. But in these moments, I realize I don't have to sit with any of these challenges alone. I notice where my mind goes and kindly, gently, firmly draw my attention back home to my body, my breath, and a loving God. A loving presence was right there with me, dwelling within my very soul and assisting me in meeting whatever my mind wanted to conjure up, whatever strong feelings arose with the thoughts. I find myself profoundly grateful for God's loving presence within me.

My body, mind, and spirit needed to learn to sit and be with whatever darkness and light existed in me. I was expending tremendous energy trying to outrun the darkness and even the intensity of so much light. Instead, I had to learn to be with rather than run away from. The only way to reduce the power of the inner darkness or the intensity of the light was to look it in the eye and welcome it in for tea.

This sounds so simple, but it can be incredibly difficult and painful. There is a reason that we run so fast and furiously away from the darkness. There is a good reason why we hustle so hard. Being with the emotional, mental, and spiritual pain inside of us is arduous. If it were easy, we would already be doing it with ease! Instead, our culture offers and encourages endless outs—we numb ourselves with food, drink, shopping, sex. We outrun our emotions with overworking, scrolling on social media, binge watching television, excessive exercise. We can even talk endlessly with friends reviewing conversations with others and hurts from long ago. While all these actions may provide a temporary solution for decreasing the pain of the present moment, they do not ease the underlying pain and wounds within.

Over time, through meditation I have learned through the Holy Spirit to sit and be with whatever past or current pain arises. I can swing open the door and welcome it in. I can swing open the door because I know I do not face my feelings and thoughts at the table alone. God is right there joining me for tea, as well.

For the longest time, I read right over the part of the Rumi poem about meeting these challenging emotions with laughter. I would open the door begrudgingly, dreading their entrance and the time I'd need to spend with them. It felt more like serving time than something in which to delight. Yet I have discovered that this spirit of welcoming with laughter is not only possible but helpful.

I found at first that I could not do the laughter part alone. My sensitive and earnest mind was too serious. I couldn't figure out how to swing the door open with a smile, much less with laughter. That is, until I turned to the help of my dear friend the Holy Spirit. The Spirit knows a great deal about playfulness and laughter. The Holy Spirit is masterful at keeping things light. When I open myself to her guidance in every situation, including when I am sitting with inner pain, a lightness eventually bubbles up. I am reminded that I don't have to figure anything out alone, which lightens the load, and with that lightness, the whole trajectory changes. When we stay grounded in strength and light, we can see situations and people from vastly more angles. When we hold things and people loosely, it gives the Holy Spirit infinitely more possibilities to enter, breathe, and shift things around.

The presence of God and the presence of the Holy Spirit allowed meditation to take on a whole new experience in my life. When I envision God sitting with me for tea along with whatever undesired emotion is present and when I allow myself to be guided by the Holy Spirit in my interaction with that emotion, meditation becomes a game changer in life. Now as I read scripture, I see in Jesus the son of a loving God who is constantly turning toward people in their pain and their joy. Even when the Pharisees are testing Jesus (and he knows it), he doesn't turn away. He stays with them. Repeatedly, Jesus sets his intention to be with those he encounters and offers presence to people, situations, and pain that society has turned away from (oftentimes justifying their turning away so as not to feel bad about it). Mindfulness can teach us how to turn toward our own pain and joy and be with it as Jesus was and continues to be with us.

Many of us need role modeling for how to be mindful and compassionate with ourselves and others. Figuring all of this out alone is difficult. Having a role model helps us visualize what it looks like to embody our faith. Even more wonderful is the ability to live an embodied faith in community. When we have people who are invested in their own and others' spiritual lives, we experience a spirit of encouragement and love. The stories of Jesus, the narratives of the saints that have followed, and the breath of the Spirit moving in real time in our everyday lives can guide us into the way, the truth, and the life moment by moment.

Being with Wholeness

Not only does meditation and mindfulness create sacred space to be with the darkness of the past, but every time something turbulent and somewhat dark enters my life, I trust I have a widened capacity to deal with it. These spiritual practices not only widen our capacity to experience and process through the darkness and pain of life, but they also widen our ability to engage laughter, love, and joy! These practices assist us in opening to the Spirit's goodness within us. We are made of the fruit of the Spirit: love, joy, peace, patience, kindness, generosity, faithfulness, gentleness, and equanimity. We're woven together in this goodness. Mindfulness has a way of helping us come home to the essence of our being, which is the fruit of the Spirit. When we can ground ourselves in our inherent inner wholeness, we not only become more compassionate and loving toward ourselves, we better love our neighbors. We become vessels of love, joy, peace, patience, kindness, generosity, faithfulness, gentleness, and equanimity.

Mindfulness has created a pathway home to myself for which I am immensely grateful. For me, life gets so crazy and hectic that I sometimes feel like a tumbleweed bouncing across the beach, tossed up into the air, floating here and there. While this can feel fun and whimsical at times, most of the time the fast pace of life simply leaves me feeling anxious, untethered, and disoriented. The more dedicated I am to a mindfulness practice, the more I find I can venture my way home. I more easily regain a connection to my breath, body, and soul simply by turning my attention to that connection. As I find my way back home to myself, I find my way home to a loving God inside me and the fruit of the Spirit that I was designed to manifest.

Learning to Kneel Before God Made Flesh

There are many ways to kneel at the feet of Jesus, whether that be walking quietly in nature, worshiping on Sunday mornings, sitting in meditation or centering prayer, reading scripture or other inspired wisdom, sharing vulnerably with an *anam cara* (soul friend), trusted friend, or spiritual companion. In all these ways of kneeling there is . . .

- allowing the breath of the Spirit to open our heart,

- allowing the breath of the Spirit to drop our mind into our heart,
- open heartedness, setting our eyes on Jesus to allow the mirror neurons to flow between us,
- allowing the breath of the Spirit to attune our soul to the God Soul,
- listening with an open heart for the wisdom of God within us, the wisdom being breathed to life by the Spirit, the wisdom being tuned by kneeling with God made flesh.

Kneeling with God made flesh allows sacred space for our soul to become still and attune to God's goodness already within us. It gives us the opportunity to remember we are always being breathed by the Spirit who is constantly tending to and renewing the inner gifts woven within us. Love, joy, peace, patience, generosity, kindness, faithfulness, gentleness, and equanimity are already crafted into every fiber and cell of our being. Kneeling with God made flesh allows us to commune with our loving God who is ever-ready and present to see, hear, and feel life with us. This simple act of kneeling with a loving God allows us to tap into who we are at our core, who we were created to be, who we deeply desire to be. Maybe it's easier than we make it to be. Maybe it's simply creating regular time to practice being with the loving God who is ever looking to be with us.

As you've already discovered, each chapter in this book ends with an invitation to practice. All of these are opportunities to kneel at Jesus' feet. At the end of the book are more practices and additional pathways that I have found support my own work. Don't give up exploring what opportunities and experiences allow you to take time to kneel at Jesus' feet and learn from his overflowing love and grace.

INVITATION TO PRACTICE: RETURNING THE MIND TO A LOVING GOD OVER AND OVER AGAIN

Sit quietly, allowing your body and mind to find some stillness. Notice how your body is meeting whatever you're sitting or lying on. Allow these sensations to ground you in the present moment. Then anchor your attention in your breath. After a few moments of gentle breathing and settling into this time and space, place a hand over your heart. Notice the sensations of your hand on your heart. Allow the weight, tenderness, and intention to bring a sense of compassion and presence to your heart space. Open your awareness to how God may be meeting you in that compassion. Imagine God turning toward your inner experience and being with you right there in this moment. Our minds drift because that is what minds do, so don't judge what your mind does organically. When you notice that your mind has drifted, choose to draw it back to your hand on your chest, your breath, and the love of God meeting you right there with whatever you are feeling. Do this practice for as long as you like. When you're ready to conclude, close with this prayer or with one of your own.

Holy and gracious God, thank you for all the ways you meet me in mind, body, and spirit. May your Spirit continue to draw my mind back to the heart of my own being where you reside. At any time, day or night, may your Spirit nudge me back into this present moment, and may I find you and your love here. Amen.

CHAPTER SEVEN

Guided by the Spirit

When the Spirit of truth comes, she will guide you into all the truth.

John 16:13

When we truly begin to accept God's favor toward us and stop hustling for God's love, it can feel overwhelming to consider what is next. What in the world will we do if we aren't preoccupied with all those rules and absorbed with feeling bad about ourselves? It might feel scary to think about living in the freedom grace offers, because it means losing many of the habits and frameworks within which we previously lived. You may get a sense of feeling unhinged and free floating, all of which can feel discombobulating and ungrounded. That doesn't sound too good. How do we harness grace to move forward with our lives? How will we sense the "right" way to live, now that we're unstuck (or even have moments of feeling unstuck) from what has previously bound us?

Enter my dear friend the Holy Spirit. I cannot remember a time when I didn't feel connected to the Holy Spirit, aware of her breath and movement in my life. As I always share in my biography, I am "a lover of the Holy Spirit." I say this because it is a description that defines the essence of my being. It's not that I have something different or special that other people don't have; I simply attuned to the Holy Spirit as a child and that attunement has grown and taken intentional shape over the years.

Just because I was attuned to the Spirit and aware of her presence didn't mean I always relied on her or had the courage to follow her guidance. When I performed with a professional children's dance company in my younger years, I suffered miserably from stage fright. Sometimes my anxiety would hit so hard that I would have sudden and paralyzing asthma attacks. One time in particular, the whole company had to stop rehearsing before a performance. I hated being the center of attention, so stopping rehearsal for my sake was miserable and shame-inducing. The director of the company had me lie on the stage and tried to help me slow my breathing down. But my lungs would not return to a normal breathing pattern, so I was taken out of the dance I was supposed to perform later that evening. After the performance was over, I vomited on the bus, relieved to be able to start breathing again, even though I was suffocating under yet another layer of shame. Years later, I wondered why I never thought to call on the Holy Spirit in those times of need. Why hadn't I asked my dear and trusted friend to breathe through me and ground me in her strength and presence? It took me years to learn the answer to that question, but I did eventually learn.

I did experience times that I could sense the presence of the Spirit, almost as if I could sense her nearness without having to remember to do so. One way I have found her wisdom appearing to me is in dreams. I experience dreams that, upon waking, inspire a sense that God was trying to tell me something. Sometimes I know what that something is, and other times, it takes pondering, sitting with, talking it over with a trusted spiritual friend to allow the meaning to be made manifest. Other times, I simply had a sense of knowing. I didn't know how I knew what I knew, but I definitely knew something—whether it was about me, my life moving forward, something from the past, other people's lives, or the world. Some may say I have a sensitive, subconscious attention to detail, but I've always felt this was a gift from the Spirit, even when the knowing doesn't feel like a gift. Sometimes it's hard to know things. Knowing isn't always enjoyable.

The dream from the beginning of the book is an example. I knew God was sharing something with me but I needed to discuss it with my spiritual director to learn more. Though it was a profound dream that was pure gift, it was not easy. I left that spiritual direction session aware that I needed to make some changes to honor the wisdom of the dream. I had a clear sense that I needed to say "no" to some things that I really would rather not say no to. It was going to cause a great deal of discomfort to put the dream into action. Yet if I was going to honor the wisdom from the dream, I was going to have to be willing to create the sacred space to come home to God rather than filling my time with obligations that crowded my calendar.

At other times, the clarity I've received in a dream has not been pleasant. In these times, it has felt like the Spirit wiping the windshield of my consciousness clean so I could see something or someone with greater clarity. Our defense mechanisms work hard during our waking hours; we block so much because it's too hard to see reality for what it actually is. Waking up to clarity that illuminates the reality of something or someone's negativity and destruction is difficult at best. We can't unknow things once they are revealed, though it may take time to integrate knowing. Again, awareness is one aspect of discomfort, then acting on that knowing with different boundaries can create a whole new level of discomfort for ourselves and the others the boundaries affect.

Through the practice of mindfulness, I have learned to hone this attunement with the Holy Spirit. I cannot exert control over the experience of her presence: she never appears on demand, as lovely as that would be. But if I can get quiet and still, I can more easily allow myself to simply be in her presence, no matter how far or near she may feel. I can trust that she is with me. I need only show reverence for this truth.

I've learned that the stillness "primes the pump" for better hearing. In the hustle of life, it can be very hard to hear the whispers of the Spirit, much less follow her wisdom. It's hard for me to stay attuned with the Spirit if I'm not spending regular time with her. She is always present with me, but I have to be intentional about remembering, knowing, trusting I'm in her presence. I've learned that the more I prioritize spending intentional time with the Spirit, the more able I am in all the other moments of my life to gain a sense of trust, knowing, and remembering.

I have to clear the clutter of my mind and heart to be able to hear and follow the Spirit. I am grateful for all the ways the Spirit finds a way into our hearts and frees us to follow her, wherever that may be. It is by her breath and guidance we are set free to live moment by moment in God's grace.

The Holy Spirit at Work in Scripture

The Holy Spirit has been making good on her name for longer than we can count. She is the movement of God in the world, the prophet whisperer, the force for good in this universe. We witness her speaking to prophets throughout the Hebrew Scriptures. In the New Testament, she fills up cousin Elizabeth, promises to fill her son John the Baptist, prophesies through Simeon, and blesses Jesus at his baptism. Jesus is led into, through, and out of the wilderness by this glorious Spirit. She appears throughout Jesus' teachings, and her presence is the promise Jesus makes to his disciples and the world. She moves in powerful ways through the book of Acts, and her work is recounted in Paul's teachings in the epistles.

A long, long time ago, long before Jesus walked the earth, the Spirit prophesied through the prophet Joel that one day she would be poured out among all people. She wouldn't reserve herself only for the prophets. She would be poured out among women and men, slaves and free, old and young. The Spirit would be unleashed onto all God's people far and wide. She would move in and through them and have her being reside within all humanity.

Jesus spoke of this before he died and again before he ascended. In the Gospel of John, he tells his followers that he must go in order for the Father to send the Spirit. It's impossible for him to teach them everything they need to learn, and it turns out that is okay, because after he leaves, the Advocate, the Holy Spirit, will be in their midst offering them guidance. This Spirit will teach them everything they need to know. Jesus promised not to leave us alone nor without a guide.

The day we celebrate as Pentecost is the day the Holy Spirit was poured out onto all God's people. It took Peter standing up and connecting the dots for everyone to comprehend their experience. Peter called back to the prophet Joel's words. He helped those gathered to see that what was happening was what had been prophesied by the prophet and promised by the Messiah. To this day, the Holy Spirit is alive and well. She comes to all of us and fills us up. She breathes new life into us and guides us forward. My experience of Pentecost is an ongoing movement of God among and within humanity. Pentecost is not a once-and-done affair. We're not simply filled up by the Holy Spirit once and set for life; the Spirit moves and breathes and has her being in and through us all the time.

The Holy Spirit's Energy in Us

Living grace is made possible, certainly easier, when we attune to the Holy Spirit's movement in our lives and in the world about us. When we're aware of being tethered to the Spirit, when we allow the Spirit to offer us wisdom and guide our lives, we are empowered to get up every morning and be an embodiment of God's love. It's easy to brush off the notion that by God's grace, God will forgive our veering from God's love and provide us what we need to live in the grace we are given. It's so very easy to say those words and not consider how God is actually doing these very things in our everyday lives. Living grace means opening ourselves to the awareness and guidance of God's active work in us by the breath of the Spirit, enlightening our minds, stirring our hearts, and strengthening our will to God's will.

The movement of God, the breath of the Spirit, does just this. The Spirit breathes through our minds and opens us to enlightenment. That great idea you had driving down the street that seemingly came out of nowhere could have been the breath of the Spirit. The awareness of your heart on fire for a certain cause or person could have been the movement of the Spirit. The courage you found to finish a project or complete what previously seemed like an impossible task could have been the Spirit offering God's strength to see you through. The times you were able to find forgiveness for someone or for yourself may have been a whisper from the Spirit, a reminder of how God has already paved the way for forgiveness. All these movements could be attributed to the Spirit working in your life.

It may be helpful to think of the Holy Spirit as the force that propels us forward, the fuel that keeps the engine moving, the wind that keeps the windmill in motion, the light that keeps our souls aflame, or the very breath that keeps us alive. When we partner with the Holy Spirit, all things are possible in God. What I love and adore about the Spirit is that she keeps coming back. She keeps showing up. We are not filled by the Spirit once and then are good to go for the rest of our lives. The Spirit keeps showing up, filling us anew, and inspiring us to move forward. She is both indwelling, already within us, and always breathing through us.

Part of this continuing to both indwell and come, renew, refill may be necessary because of our nature of continual growth. Jesus told the disciples that their grieving hearts couldn't fit too much more in before he ascended; they couldn't bear it. Part of the humility of being human is that we're a constant work in progress. There is only so much we can learn at any one time and truly integrate within our minds and beings. So the Spirit keeps showing up. She's a lovely companion that way. Her wisdom is infinite, and her teachings are endless.

Mary's Reliance on the Holy Spirit

As we've already begun to explore, Mary, the mother of Jesus, is a powerful example of what it looks like to partner with the Holy Spirit. Repeatedly through the nativity story, she allows the Holy Spirit to move through her, and she also notes when the Spirit is moving through others as well. The angel Gabriel shares with Mary that if she says yes to the plan of bearing God's son, the Holy Spirit would be the one to make it so. When she visits her older cousin, Elizabeth is filled with the Holy Spirit and exclaims Mary's truth. When John the Baptist is born to Elizabeth, his father, Zechariah the priest, is filled with the Holy Spirit and prophesied about his son and The Messiah to follow him. When Jesus is taken to Jerusalem to be presented to the Lord (as was custom for all males), a holy man named Simeon is guided by the Spirit to speak about Jesus. He even says to Mary, "a sword will pierce your own soul too."

It's no wonder that Mary ponders so many things within her heart. Between her own encounters with angels and the Spirit together with the holy encounters of those dear to her, there is much to take in and consider. Mary takes the time to weave together all the messages from God about her son. She has a treasure trove of love notes from God, even if some of the messages are particularly scary. The notes stitched together are adding up to something quite extraordinary.

I wonder if these encounters with the angels and being filled with the Spirit are what sustain her when it's so hard to make sense of her son, his ministry, and divinity mixed with humanity. When Jesus was twelve and stayed behind in Jerusalem without his parents' knowing, they looked for him for three terrifying, anxiety-filled days while he was sitting among the teachers, listening and asking questions. Mary gets after Jesus (like most anxiety-ridden mothers do with their fear provoking twelve-year-old sons!), and he simply replies, "Why were you searching for me? Did you not know that I must be in my Father's house?"

The scripture says that they didn't understand what he was saying to them. It makes sense that they didn't understand. In their mind, he wasn't in his father's house and neither had they been in their house. They had spent the past three days pulling their hair out looking for their lost preteen. Though Mary doesn't understand what Jesus has said, she also doesn't throw his words away. Rather, she "treasured all these things in her heart." It's as if she is collecting sea glass along the beach; sea glass that is intimately connected to her son's life. She places these difficult to understand words and experiences in the pouch of her heart. She treasures them. She holds them dear. She allows herself to be with them with God. She knows or maybe simply senses all these pieces of sea glass are adding up to something astonishing.

It is so easy to forget that we too are visited by angels and filled with the Holy Spirit. We can also glean wisdom and put together pieces of sea glass. If we simply stand still and consider the pieces of holy sea glass we've already put away in the pouch of our hearts, we too might realize that the Spirit has been breathing through us and our lives and through the lives of those around us as well. It may even be creating something breathtaking and exceptional. I've been collecting holy sea glass most of my life, and I try to stay curious about what God is making of my life.

The Holy Spirit in Jesus' Life

We can learn much about the movement of the Spirit for our own lives by paying attention to how the Spirit showed up in Jesus' life. In the Gospel of Luke, chapter 4 begins with "Jesus, full of the Holy Spirit, returned from the Jordan and was led by the Spirit in the wilderness, where for forty days he was tested by the devil." For most of my life, I glossed over what this verse actually says and assumed that the devil led Jesus into the wilderness. When I read it more closely and understood what it truly said, I was shocked. My dearest friend, the Holy Spirit, led Jesus into the wilderness?

As I slowed down my reading and opened my heart, what the Holy Spirit was up to began to make more sense. Right before this guidance into the wilderness is the glorious moment of Jesus' baptism in the Jordan River. It is a powerfully divine moment, where the Spirit alights on Jesus like a dove, the voice of God calls Jesus beloved, and Jesus is baptized in the Jordan River by the hands of John the Baptist. All three persons of the Trinity, in addition to the human hands of John the Baptist, unite to mark the significance of the moment and, in doing so, set the stage for the importance of our baptisms.

In his baptism, Jesus is filled with the Holy Spirit. We may even think of this as a major attunement with the Spirit and love of God in one miraculous moment. It is from there that Jesus is driven into the wilderness. I've come to think of this wilderness time as an opportunity to test drive the power of baptism. What good is the power of the Holy Spirit within us if we don't know what that power enables us to do or be? Jesus being both human and divine would be fully aware and equipped to manage the power of the Spirit within him; we have to keep remembering that his life, ministry, death, and resurrection were to teach us about our lives in God. We needed a living, breathing example of how to live our human lives in the divine covenant with God. We needed an example with flesh that we could observe and witness; we needed an example of how to live in right relationship with God. So much of Jesus' time in the wilderness gives us instruction and inspiration on how we are to handle temptation and difficulties in our own lives. Through Jesus' example of being empowered by the Holy Spirit in the wilderness, we learn how to meet the turbulent, oftentimes lonely wilderness stretches we encounter.

The Gospel of Luke shares that Jesus eventually leaves the wilderness and, again, filled with the Holy Spirit begins his ministry. It's the Spirit that fills and empowers him, leads him into and through the wilderness, then fills and sends him out into the world for ministry. Was this wilderness time necessary before starting his ministry? Could he have moved from baptism to ministry without the testing of the wilderness? My experience has taught me that the movement of the Spirit is always to offer us the goodness of God, even when the experience causes pain. I'm not one to believe that God causes bad things to happen in our lives; I think humanity and life in general serve those up quite naturally without any divine help. I do sense that whatever life or someone throws me, the Spirit can teach me something through the experience. She can breathe through me and other people; she can breathe through the situation itself and offer wisdom and learning that I couldn't have gotten otherwise. It's been through the tough experiences in my life that I've learned to receive the gifts of the Spirit as I need them.

Making Space for the Spirit

The Letter to the Galatians says that "the fruit of the Spirit is love, joy, peace, patience, kindness, generosity, faithfulness, gentleness, and self-control . . . If we live by the Spirit, let us also be guided by the Spirit." The fruit of the Spirit rolls out almost like a Hallmark card; there is such a sweetness to each of these offerings. And yet the moments when I have really known these gifts have been the more difficult moments when I needed these offerings most. For example, when I think back over the years of parenting my two sons, it has been the times I lacked patience that I have yearned for it the most, the moments when I thought I was losing my mind that somehow, by the grace of God, the Spirit offered me patience so that I had patience to extend to my children. It has been during the times when I have been rip roaring mad about something and wanted to tear through someone that the Spirit has handed me an olive branch of peace or gentleness just before I opened my mouth with flames.

Mindfulness teaches us to observe our mind, our body, our emotions. We notice all these through following the feelings and sensations of the body. As we continue to practice mindfulness, we find that, in time, even when we're not actively in meditation, we're more aware of ourselves—our thoughts, feelings, and emotions—so that when we're moving about our daily lives and we become reactive, a little space opens up to actually be aware of those feelings and sensations of reactivity. With this awareness, a world of possibility opens to us. I call it the miracle of a split second. I've come to think of this little gap as a space to let the Holy Spirit in, just enough space to slow me down and open me to whatever gift the Spirit might serve all those present—love, joy, peace, patience, kindness, generosity, faithfulness, gentleness, and self-control. Because at the end of the day, aren't we all simply trying to be agents of the Holy Spirit? Isn't that how we breathe new life into our families, friendships, communities, workplaces, and world? When love, joy, peace, patience, kindness, generosity, faithfulness, gentleness, and equanimity have space to flow between us, that's when the kingdom of God becomes real in our midst. We'll discuss the gifts of the Spirit throughout following chapters with a main focus on them again in the last chapter.

The remaining chapters will highlight how we come home to grace by staying aligned with the Holy Spirit and following her lead, noticing how she enlightens our minds, stirs our hearts, and strengthens our will to follow God's will. The final chapter will share how the Spirit grows the fruits of the Spirit within us, allowing for resurrected living in our daily lives. The Spirit weaves not only through our individual lives but also in our collective lives as well. The Spirit has a way of enlivening whole communities and guiding them forward into God's goodness for the community itself as well as the greater good of the world.

INVITATION TO PRACTICE: GUIDED BY THE SPIRIT

Sit quietly, allowing your body and mind to find some stillness. Notice how your body is meeting whatever you're sitting or lying on. Allow these sensations to ground you in the present moment. Then anchoring your attention in your breath, open your awareness to how your breath is infinitely connected to the movement of God, the breath of the Spirit. You may want to intentionally invite the Spirit to breathe through your mind, your thoughts, your thought patterns. Remember that the Spirit can be called upon to guide your thoughts at any time. After several breath cycles, invite the Spirit to breathe through your heart space. Allow the Spirit to nourish your heart. Allow the Spirit to be present to and with any emotions you are experiencing or have experienced recently. After several breath cycles, invite the Spirit to drop into your gut, to breathe through your gut instincts. Allow this holy breath to nourish your intuition, your sense of knowing. Notice how the breath of the Spirit nourishes your whole being—body, mind, soul, and spirit. From this holy breath, the Spirit guides you. When you're ready to conclude this practice, end with this prayer or with one of your own.

Holy and gracious God, thank you for releasing your Advocate into our beings. Thank you for all the ways she both grounds and guides us in our everyday lives. As I move through this day or settle into this night, may my mind, heart, gut, and soul be guided by the loving breath of the Spirit. Amen.

CHAPTER EIGHT

Enlightening Our Minds and Stirring Our Hearts

When Herod died, an angel of the Lord suddenly appeared in a dream to Joseph in Egypt and said, 'Get up, take the child and his mother, and go to the land of Israel, for those who were seeking the child's life are dead.' Then Joseph got up, took the child and his mother, and went to the land of Israel. But when he heard that Archelaus was ruling over Judea in place of his father Herod, he was afraid to go there. And after being warned in a dream, he went away to the district of Galilee. There he made his home in a town called Nazareth, so that what had been spoken through the prophets might be fulfilled, 'He will be called a Nazarene.'

MATTHEW 2:19-23

They said to each other, "Were not our hearts burning
within us

while he was talking to us on the road, while he was opening the scriptures to us?"

LUKE 24:32

Spirit Enlightening Our Minds

For years, I was in the miserable throes of discerning whether to divorce; I was tormented by doubt. I had so many good reasons to leave the marriage, and I could come up with so many, many reasons to stay. I felt like I was in a perpetual windstorm being thrown back and forth as my mind wrestled how to move forward. I was absolutely distraught. One day, I was meeting with a dear mentor, and she shared with me that clearly it wasn't time to decide yet. The torment I was experiencing was a sign of the lack of any peace. She assured me that one day I would have peace about a decision. I would "know."

At the time, I couldn't imagine knowing, certainly with any sense of peace. That began my new round of torment. I allowed myself to feel devastated by a lack of knowing and the fierce doubt that I would ever know with peace. Yet I did find comfort in my mentor's words. She offered those words with such an ease in her being; she offered them with her own sense of lived knowing, drawing from the wisdom of her life experience.

Weeks, months, maybe it was even a year later, I had a dream. In the dream, I was in a brightly lit restaurant talking with someone who was telling me that they had spent eight years in their marriage and it was time to leave it. This person was kind and thoughtful, incredibly peaceful and self-assured, confident. As they spoke, I could feel the rightness of the decision. When I woke up, I could feel God's presence and blessing in the dream.

Later that same day, I was talking to a close friend on the phone via a bluetooth headset as I drove. They said to me, "If you need to leave your marriage, it's okay." I almost ran off the road hearing these words coming into my ears. This person didn't even know that I had been wrestling with this decision; I had never spoken of it with them. What were the chances of having this peaceful dream that felt like a divine blessing, the knowing I had been waiting for woven with the peace I yearned for, and then to have this live voice affirm what I'd heard in the dream? My mind felt enlightened.

Though the ensuing days and weeks, months, and years were anything but easy, that dream and affirmation immediately afterward were a profound rock for me. It became a spiritual touchstone that returned me home again and again to both myself and to my loving God. It grounded me and kept me steady when the pain overwhelmed me, when the tears came unbidden, when the single parenting bedtime routine exhausted me beyond my limits. I could ground myself in the peace of knowing offered to me that day by a loving God through a dream and a friend, guiding me home through peaceful enlightenment.

The Spiritual Practice of Waiting

Oftentimes, we don't wait on God's direction before we act. We don't practice enough patience awaiting the guidance of the Holy Spirit. Our pain or anxiety gets the best of us and propels us into action before receiving a holy nod. Our work is to open ourselves to the enlightenment of God, open our hearts to God's stirring, and wait. We think that if we have enough discipline to use our agency to turn toward God and open to God's direction, God will meet us in that very moment of faithful, intentional connection with answers, ease, peace, clarity. We can become irritated and impatient when we then have to wait in an open stance, which leaves us quite vulnerable.

Opening ourselves to God's direction and the guidance of the Holy Spirit is vulnerable. Staying open while we just hang out waiting on God usually requires having to feel our feelings rather than numb or avoid the pain. It means facing the anxiety of the unknown and trusting, as Julian of Norwich prayed, that *all will be well* even if we have no possible idea how that might look.

Our practice of faith is in both the discipline of opening and the patience of waiting. Each year, the season of Advent gives us practice for intentional waiting. In this season, we wait and wait and wait some more for the birth of Jesus. Most children, of course, feel as if they are waiting for Santa. And they are, but they are also waiting to celebrate the birth of the Christ child into the world anew, remembering the act of God's grace thousands of years ago and the anticipation of his coming again. As Christians, we are a people of disciplined waiting and a people of action.

The faster society moves, the quicker our internet runs, the fuller our lives become, the greater our need to practice waiting. We don't wait for food in a fast-food world. We don't wait for rain with irrigation and sprinklers. We don't wait for a nudge from the Holy Spirit when we can consult Google or Siri. For the most part, we have eliminated waiting from our lives.

Yet there are some huge aspects of life that always will require waiting. Waiting for a child to be born. Waiting on the "right one" to marry. We cannot strong-arm fate. We cannot orchestrate divine intervention. We cannot conjure up a burning bush of God's presence.

The True Mover and Shaker of Our Lives

Our spiritual lives remind us that we are not the true movers and shakers of our lives. As much as we might want to find "the one," fall in love, and begin the rest of our lives in romantic bliss, we cannot make that person appear. There is some element of fate involved. As much as I wanted to be done with pregnancy, I had to wait on my body's readiness to give birth and my child's readiness to be born. As much as I wanted to get published years ago, the stars didn't align until this book.

We live in a culture, however, that teaches us that we are the instruments of our own destiny. To some extent, that is accurate. We can and need to use our agency for good. But we must also allow God, Jesus, the Holy Spirit to meet us and be co-creators with us, which means working on their time and in their flow.

There are many wonderful examples of God enlightening people in the Bible. For example, Joseph, upon learning that Mary is pregnant, considers walking away, given that she's pregnant and he hasn't had sexual relations with her. Just as he has resolved to leave Mary, an angel comes to him in a dream and tells him not to walk away but to marry her, for she is to give birth to God's son. When Joseph awakes, he puts aside his own plan and pursues the direction given to him by the angel.

Luckily for Joseph, the angel appears again, this time sharing how to keep his son safe from King Herod, who is out to destroy him. The angel tells Joseph to take Mary and Jesus and flee to Egypt and remain there until further notice, which he does. When Herod dies, the angel again appears in another dream and gives Joseph new directions, to go to Judea. As Joseph is carrying out this last direction, he becomes scared. In yet another dream, he is directed to go to Galilee instead, where they finally settle as a family in Nazareth.

As a sister in faith and a spiritual companion, I would love to ask Joseph questions about his dreams. Did he awake from any of his dreams with questions? Did he have to reason anything out? Did he have doubts about what to do or from whom the guidance came? How did he know it was an angel of the Lord? Did he ever wonder if he was going crazy? Did he question whether it was good advice, if the guidance truly would save his child? Did he talk the dreams over with Mary before setting out each time? What, if anything, gave him the assurance needed to act on how he was directed each time? And what was with the blip about Judea—did the angel direct him incorrectly that time, did he misunderstand, or did human actions change in a way that meant the holy family needed new directions from the angel to get to where they ultimately needed to go? What would have happened had he not felt that fear arise within him?

The Spirit Meets Us in Mindfulness

One of the exciting things I've discovered about my faith over the last several years is that it is meant to be lived—*embodied.* I can read about it, mull it over, pray about it, and discuss it with friends, but at the end of the day, the call on my life (and I believe the call on humanity) is to *embody* the goodness we profess with our lips. We must put our study and words into action. The way we do that is through spiritual practices. These practices prime our minds and our bodies to be ready to act when the Spirit calls us to.

As you've likely surmised, a practice that has been especially meaningful to me is meditation, or mindfulness. As I leaned into learning mindfulness and breath work, I found myself with a greater capacity to connect with a loving God and with the breath of the Holy Spirit. I started with whatever I could handle—five minutes here, thirty seconds there, eight minutes at a particular time of day, and slowly I built up to twenty minutes.

Though I am a profound introvert who craves and adores silence, being quiet did not translate to my mind being quiet. In fact, I think sometimes I crave quiet just so I can hear my mind amidst the clatter of the world. I yearn to hear the still small voice within not only among the loudness of the world but even more so within the whirlwind of my own mind.

People always think mindfulness is about getting the mind to be quiet and blank for long stretches of time. This is not so. Mindfulness is about knowing where your mind is in any given moment. Have you ever driven somewhere familiar and you arrive having no memory of getting there, your mind lost in thought the whole time? Not only do you not remember seeing anything as you drove the familiar path, you also don't remember what you were thinking about. Most of us move through our lives on automatic pilot with no idea what we're thinking about or paying attention to as we go.

Mindfulness is setting an intention to notice where our mind is in any moment. Many meditation teachers have added "non-judgmentally" to this description—noticing where our mind is at any moment non-judgmentally. "Non-judgmentally" is usually the kicker. As soon as we notice where our mind is and what's going on or realize our mind has drifted somewhere we didn't intend, we have opinions about it. We get reactive or frustrated with our lack of mindfulness. But this is also part of mindfulness: learning to be in the present moment, whatever is happening, whatever we're thinking, whatever we're feeling, just as we are, without opinions and reactivity,

I believe the Holy Spirit is yearning to meet us in every moment. Why would the Spirit yearn to meet us in every moment? What is the theology around the Holy Spirit yearning to meet us with every breath? Well, first, Jesus said he'd send an Advocate to guide us into all truth. Just as God offered us Jesus, Emmanuel, "God with us," God offers us an ongoing advocate and guide who is "God with us." When I take an honest look within and a "head out of the sand" look around the world, I'm thinking God sees the need for us to constantly be checking in with this divine, benevolent guide, the Holy Spirit. So, how do we do it? How do we check in with and stay connected to the

Spirit? How do we allow the Spirit to guide us? Mindfulness practices have been instrumental for me in this work.

Readying for Enlightenment

Though I meditate regularly, I will tell you that I have rarely experienced my mind being enlightened while sitting on my beloved meditation cushion. In fact, I can only think of one time—one!—where I have had a stroke of insight, understanding, or enlightenment while in practice. Before you run off with an unintended permission slip to give up on meditation, what I also know is that regular meditation has widened my capacity for experiencing enlightenment more often in other parts of my life.

When I stick to the discipline of meditation or centering prayer, the practice quiets my mind, my body, and my soul. The Holy Spirit meets me in the stillness and quiet and does some housecleaning. As I breathe in and out and allow myself to settle and come home to myself, I do sense the Spirit clearing out the cobwebs that have built up in the frenetic movement of my life. She sweeps away the debris and mud that has begun to cover my heart and maybe even caused some toxicity in my mind. After the practice, I sense I'm a more decluttered vessel that is better able to receive the whispers of the Spirit. I sense I'm more open to recognizing enlightenment when it occurs. Meditation and centering prayer ready me to receive from the Spirit and sense her movement within me.

Talking Enlightenment Through

Another practice that connects me to the Spirit is talking with specific people. Oftentimes in my own life, I have to talk things through with a wise counselor, a trusted friend, my own spiritual companion, or my partner.

I've had several times when I've awoken from a dream and had a sense that I'd just experienced a God dream. God was clearly trying to tell me something. Sometimes I knew instantly, instinctively, what that something was that God wanted me to see/know/understand; other times, I've awoken knowing it was a God dream but not had a clue as to what it meant. I couldn't crack the code. It took time, reflection, and a trusted community within which to talk it out. I had to allow God's message time and space to come to light in its own accord, and it did so through my conversations with others.

One example of this is the dream I shared at the opening of this book, the dream of my dream home being torn down. The next morning after this dream, I met with my spiritual companion and I told her about the dream. I was just talking, reflecting on the dream without thinking too much about what I was saying. She stopped me at one point (which is very uncharacteristic of her) and said, "Caroline, you've said that three times now. *I have to take as much off my calendar as I can.* You've said it three times." I literally hadn't heard myself. I sensed what the dream was telling me, but I was drowning out the immediate directions. I likely didn't want to hear the specifics or consider what that would mean to put the guidance into action. I didn't want to flee to Egypt. I didn't want to head to Israel only to find myself frightened and have to move again.

To date, I have yet to change geographic locations due to directions in a dream. But, as you now know from this chapter, I have left a marriage supported by a blessing from God I received in a dream. I've left a job that I really rather loved after direction from a dream. I've known the song of my heart better from dreams and been led into the wilderness by the Spirit through a dream. I know dreams are not how God enlightens everyone's minds. It's only one of so many, many ways God whispers to us and the Spirit breathes enlightenment into our minds, but it is often the way I experience God working in my life.

All the ways I have experienced God's grace enlightening my mind have been obvious in that there wasn't a way that I could have orchestrated the enlightenment myself. We cannot strong-arm knowing. There is always a stroke of benevolence that feels beyond my created reach. I've experienced the enlightenment of my mind by sitting in a twelve-step meeting and hearing the very thing I needed to hear to help me realize "the next right thing." I've taken walks with friends who have shared a story of their own life that lit the path for my own journey. There have been moments of enlightenment about my own life when I've read insights characters have in novels. There have been oodles of times when something a mentor, therapist, or spiritual director has shared enlightened my mind. I lost count a long time ago how many times my children have enlightened my mind to God's wisdom from the backseat of the car. Their curiosity and openness helped crack my mind open to see things differently and more broadly, offering new perspectives. I've also experienced enlightenment driving down the road following the usual path I take Monday through Friday, driving my children to school and then myself to work. In the pure, beautiful silence in my car driving along, suddenly there can be an insight of clarity, and my mind feels enlightened.

Pondering Enlightenment with a Group

Sometimes I wonder how often God is trying to enlighten us and we're just too busy to notice or care. How might we experience the Spirit descending upon us in unison? How would we know it was happening? Are there times when we might be experiencing the Spirit descend upon people before our very eyes?

I recently led a retreat based on the contents of this book. It was a thoughtful, kind, engaged, soulful, intelligent group of women who were collectively pondering the love of God and how we experience this love in palpable ways. Together, we wondered how do we know when God is enlightening our minds by grace? One woman shared about how she has to practice coming home to the enlightenment. Another woman chimed in that it took intention to pay attention. Over the weekend, we noticed that these two pieces of wisdom kept arising. We have to both be intentional and practice. It takes some effort. We can't assume enlightenment is just going to come like a lightening bolt in the sky (though sometimes it can). Enlightenment is more about making the space to come home to our loving God with practice and intention and in that sacred connection noticing what arises.

One of the many reasons I love leading retreats is that it gives people the opportunity to hear one another's inner experience, thoughts, ideas, and emotions within a safe and sacred environment. I adore watching people's faces as they share with a depth of authenticity and integrity, the tenderness in their face, the vulnerability in their voice, oftentimes the tears in their eyes. They are using sacred space to say something aloud that matters to them. They are allowing themselves the opportunity to be seen in a meaningful way by people who are on the journey too. Something else I find profound is watching the ones who are listening to what is being shared, noticing an "aha" come across their face, a knowing smile settle on their lips, that soulful recognition of the common humanity being articulated for everyone, even if the specifics are different.

We learn so much from listening to one another. Listening circles and good retreats are a both/and. They offer the opportunity to both see and be seen, hear and be heard in soulful, connective, meaningful ways. In a gathering of intentional people, the Spirit has endless ways to awaken the mind and bring enlightenment.

Whether collectively or individually, we are invited to move through our days experiencing the love of God in our midst. We can be intentional and practice attuning our minds to the inherent wisdom within. We can build trust within ourselves and with God that the wisdom within us is actually from God. We can practice spiritual disciplines each day where we get quiet, still, and lean into that benevolent presence. The Spirit's presence is just waiting to breathe wisdom in a way we can hear, feel, sense, see. Oftentimes, the enlightenment we need for this day is simply on the other side of a meditation session, a walk with a friend, or a session with a spiritual companion. Intention and practice can allow us to trust the words of Jesus that indeed he sent an Advocate to guide us into all truth and she is already here already breathing within us. Breathing us into enlightenment.

Spirit Stirring Our Hearts

I've had several times in my life when I felt God gave me knowledge that affected my decisions or benefited me in some way. Some of these came through dreams, as I've shared. Others just came as some sense of understanding. I couldn't make sense of how I knew what I knew. I just knew. Most of these times have been a knowing about something inherently good or positive. A few times, I've known about something that wasn't good. Either way, the knowing was most beneficial if I could stay with it and allow the Spirit to breathe through it as I tried to make sense of the knowledge and understand how it should be incorporated into my life.

When I was applying to divinity schools, I sensed a knowing of where I wanted to go. It felt like more than a desire to attend a particular school; the choice of the school felt somehow yoked with a stirring in my heart. I didn't think I had any chance of getting in to this school. I had always studied and worked hard in school, successfully completing high school, an undergraduate degree, and a master's degree in counseling, but I was never the best test taker or the quickest with facts. (I hate playing *Trivial Pursuit*!)

Yet I had a stirring in my heart to at least go visit this school. While I was there, I felt like the Spirit just kept gently opening doors by introducing me to people. When I first arrived, I was to meet with someone in the admissions office. Upon entering this woman's office, she began explaining how she shouldn't have gotten my email but somehow did; it "should have" gone to another admissions officer. Once she read my email, however, she knew she was the one to meet with me. We had so much to talk about! I left her office an hour later feeling so grateful that she had somehow received my email and that I was able to meet with her. Regardless of whether I got in, I felt like I was supposed to meet her, as our connection to each other had been strong.

Before I had arrived for the visit, I had reached out to a couple of professors that I especially wanted to meet while there. One professor in particular hadn't returned my email, so I figured she was too busy to schedule a meeting. During my visit, I went to the bookstore, and the manager of the store was so kind and started a conversation with me. In the natural conversation about what I hoped to do while visiting the campus, I mentioned I'd wanted to meet this certain professor, and she said, "Oh, she's teaching in the next room over. I'll introduce you when her class releases in a few minutes." I couldn't believe my "luck" or this woman's generosity. Not only did she introduce me, but the professor invited me to walk back to her office with her to chat. We walked across campus to her office, and I had the opportunity to share why I was excited to take her classes if admitted to the school. We had an amazing conversation, and before I left, she called the admissions office and told them I had her vote for acceptance. I was speechless.

When I returned home, my mind kept doubting my chances of getting in, but my heart kept burning. I purchased boots for the northeastern winter. My mother cautioned such a purchase given that I hadn't been accepted. The boots became an outward sign of the inner grace of my stirred heart. Months later, when the large envelope arrived in the mail, I was speechless yet again. I got in. Somehow the stirring in my heart, the knowing of where I was going to school, was made manifest.

The boots came in very handy for far too many months each year I was there. Acceptance letters and boots may not seem like a big deal, but when I look back over the first fifty years of my life, attending divinity school was not only one of my favorite stretches of time, it was also life changing for me.

Over the years, I have pondered about other times when I thought I knew something, but I didn't—the times I was mistaken. Unlike divinity school, I did not get into my first or second choice of colleges, and I came close to transferring my junior year of college because I wasn't happy; though I had made some wonderful friends, the college I attended didn't feel like a good fit. College felt like a wilderness time for me. There wasn't much about the four-year experience that stirred my heart at all. Though I trust the Spirit was with me, she was rarely palpable. I felt more like bouncing tumbleweed than someone guided by the Spirit. As much as I have always wanted the Spirit's presence to be clear and palpable at all times, she hasn't been. I accept this as part of the human condition. I have learned there are genuinely times when the Spirit's presence is hard to detect or understand, and other times that it is only in retrospect that we can see and appreciate the movement of the Spirit.

Burning Hearts

I love the story of the two men walking to Emmaus after Passover in Luke 24. They are returning home with heavy hearts after witnessing the death of Jesus on the cross. They are still dumbfounded by the empty tomb. As they walk, they are talking together, trying to make sense of all they have experienced. Jesus comes along and falls in step with them, though they don't recognize the man walking beside them as Jesus. This fellow road companion asks questions about what they are discussing. They are bewildered that anyone remotely close to Jerusalem would not have heard all that happened to Jesus of Nazareth.

Jesus tells them, "Oh, how foolish you are and how slow of heart to believe all that the prophets declared!" (verse 25). Even then, they do not see him for who he really is. Jesus starts connecting the dots for them. He rewinds the tape all the way to Moses and reveals how the scriptures piece together the story of God's plan and the life, death, and resurrection of the Messiah. Still the men don't fully see what he's revealing because they still don't recognize Jesus.

When they get close to town, Jesus walks on ahead of them, but the men call after him and ask him to stay with them. As they are at the table together, Jesus "took bread, blessed and broke it, and gave it to them. Then their eyes were opened, and they recognized him, and he vanished from their sight" (v. 30-31). Their hearts are finally opened to see what their physical eyes could not. The two men look at each other and say, "Were not our hearts burning within us while he was talking to us on the road, while he was opening the scriptures to us?" They immediately return to Jerusalem to tell the other disciples what they have seen.

This story is a beautiful description of God stirring the heart. At the center are two humble people who have just witnessed the death of Jesus. They've heard the news of the women reporting the tomb was empty. They are walking along trying to make sense of an experience that makes no sense whatsoever. Even Jesus comes along and guides their minds in putting all the puzzle pieces together—he connects the dots through scripture and history, and still, they cannot see the big picture. They cannot see that it is Jesus before them as the Risen Messiah, nor can they see how the scriptures reveal the possibility for a risen Messiah.

It takes a physical act of Jesus to open the eyes of their heart. It takes the embodiment of God's love through the breaking of bread for them to understand their stirred hearts. It's as if the information Jesus has given them drops from their head to their hearts, and there the true mind (the mind of the heart) is opened through the embodiment of love.

Jesus breaks bread with them as he did with many during his ministry and as he did with the disciples at the Last Supper. Here we have Jesus once again exemplifying the power of this meal, sharing the essence of his being through bread and wine, physically handing it to these men, and their eyes are opened.

Not only are their eyes opened, but they also get honest with themselves. They play back the day and realize that indeed their hearts were burning within them while Jesus spoke to them on the road. God had stirred their hearts, but their minds hadn't yet understood what this stirring meant. It is only after the fact that they even acknowledge that their hearts were burning within them as they had been walking the road with Jesus.

How often do we do this too? When the eyes of our heart are opened to something, it can cause us to look back and realize something has been stirring in us all along. We can work to become more awake and aware of when God is stirring our hearts. Maybe there had been glimpses of stirring on the road to Emmaus while Jesus was speaking, and neither man took the time or space to breathe into that stirring. When we work to attune our hearts to God, we can grow our ability to sense when God is stirring something in us and train our bodies to take deep breaths and receive the movement we experience.

It is natural to want to quickly understand what is stirring in our hearts. When we become aware of God's guidance within us, we often want to be able to act on that stirring pretty quickly. Yet our first faithful posture is to simply be with the stirring of the heart, to notice it is happening. We must allow ourselves to be curious about the stirring, to sit and breathe with the stirring without rushing to understand. Forcing our minds to understand what God is stirring in us causes us to move too fast and act too quickly on God's work, instead of letting God do the work in God's time. We can show reverence to the stirring by breathing into the stirring and turning our attention to God in a posture of reception. We can pray, meditate, or simply breathe. The point is to sit and receive, not to rush to act.

A Cautious Burn of the Heart

Some stirrings are easier to lean into than others. We think of our hearts burning within us to share something "good." We look forward to God trying to get our attention to share something that we're going to find pleasing and positive.

But I've also experienced times when I felt my heart was burning within me as a warning regarding danger. The feelings and sensations in my body registered that something was amiss or someone wasn't who they presented to be—darkness masquerading as the light, a wolf in sheep's clothing. As someone who has always tried to see the good in all people and in all situations, this has been a hard spiritual lesson for me to learn. I think it can be an arduous spiritual lesson for many Christians to learn. Sometimes the Spirit stirs our heart with a knowing to protect us, but acknowledging this requires us to accept that not all people have good intentions and not all situations are inherently good.

Many of us are trained to address the stirrings of our hearts only when our rational mind can make sense of them. We tend to trust and respect stirs that make all the data points align or confirm what we already think or believe (or want to believe). We're generally taught not to trust the stirrings of our hearts unless we can make total sense of what they mean. However, the Spirit often offers us wisdom in ways that take time and sometimes effort to comprehend, much less appreciate and honor. In my experience, the Spirit often offers deeper wisdom than initially meets the eye.

It has been through hard inner work and having the privilege of journeying alongside others that I have grown tremendous appreciation for how hard it can be to listen and trust the enlightenment of our minds and/or stirring of our hearts. Many of us have experienced small "t" or large "T" traumas that prevent our ability to track meaningful stirs in our hearts and minds because trauma taught us that to listen and honor that tracking would prove dangerous. So, in so many cases, it is no small feat to attune to the movement of the Spirit and find our way into following her guidance.

Opening of the Heart

The thing about our hearts being stirred is the need for our hearts to be open for that stir to occur. A certain amount of space is needed for a good stir. When my heart is closed off in fear and trepidation or when I'm locked down trembling, it is hard for the Holy Spirit to have any space to move and breathe and have her being within my heart. Again, the tools of meditation and centering prayer can be incredibly useful in settling and clearing my heart so that I might be open enough for the Spirit to move in me.

That said, I have also experienced times when no practice seemed to help. Sometimes, I must ask the Spirit to open my heart and to stir. She rarely responds on demand, yet she always shows up—eventually. One time, I told my beloved spiritual director that I feared God was going to drop me. Sure, God had brought me through challenges before, but I was afraid there would come a time when God would drop me. I wondered, *what then?* As I shared this concern, I felt sure my spiritual director would tell me that God would never, ever drop me, that she would attempt to reassure my fears with assurances of God's faithfulness. Instead, she replied, "You'll be fine. You'll bounce." I immediately started laughing. I realized God was taking care of whatever situation might arise ahead of time: God would continue to catch me when I feared falling, and God had designed me to bounce, so I'd be fine that way too. Whether I use my tools to open myself to the Spirit's movement in my life or to encourage my waiting on God's guidance, one way or another, the grace of God always reaches me.

INVITATION TO PRACTICE: ACKNOWLEDGING SPIRIT'S MOVEMENT AND BEING WITH IT

As you sit in prayerful meditation, make space to acknowledge and be with your heart. Allow yourself time and space to notice if you've had any feelings in your heart over the last 24 hours or previous week. Give yourself time to build the muscle of paying attention to your heart. (So many of us zoom by our hearts we don't even realize they're being stirred.) Regardless of whether you sense a stir within your heart, the simple act of being with our hearts, coming home to our own hearts is a spiritual practice in and of itself. It builds a willingness and capacity to be with that which God has made, pours into, and stirs within us. So, even if nothing comes, allow yourself the time to simply be with your heart. If you sense or recognize a stirring, you might say a small prayer: *I feel you stirring my heart, God. In your time, may I understand this stirring and have the courage to act on it.*

You can also use a breath prayer: as you breathe in, say, "I sense you stirring my heart, O Lord." And as you breathe out, say, "May I make room for this stirring."

Or use a simpler breath prayer: Inbreath: *God is stirring.* Outbreath: *Making room to receive.*

Or even simpler: Inbreath: *Stirring.* Outbreath: *Receiving.*

When our faith is about living in connection with God every moment of the day, every breath of our lives, it's about a willingness to breathe with whatever God is offering us in mind, body, and spirit. You can end your practice with the following prayer or one you choose.

Holy and gracious God, thank you for all the times you have enlightened my mind and stirred my heart whether I have known it was you or not. In this moment, receive my gratitude for the Spirit's movement. This day (or night), may I honor your wisdom within me and be willing to continue to receive your guidance through the enlightenment of my mind and the stirring of my heart. Amen.

CHAPTER NINE

Strengthening Our Will to Flow in God's Will

Three times I appealed to the Lord about this, that it would leave me, but he said to me, 'My grace is sufficient for you, for power is made perfect in weakness.' So, I will boast all the more gladly of my weaknesses, so that the power of Christ may dwell in me.

2 Corinthians 12:8-9

I get nervous when anyone starts talking about "the will of God." Who actually knows the will of God? Who is so presumptuous to even think they might have a grasp on God's will? So much of understanding the will of God is interpretation, discernment, and opinion. So I tread lightly as I move into a chapter exploring our will and God's will. Yet I know we need not throw the baby out with the bathwater and say that if no one can really know God's will, why even discuss it. At the heart of my belief system is a loving God who desires health, goodness, and connection with all of us. Whatever God's will is, I deeply believe it is good for us, good for our neighbors, good for all of creation. It might not always—or ever—be easy to know or follow, yet it is inherently good and whole.

As humans, we have a tendency to get busy judging others based on whether they are following God's will or not, and that always means following what the self-appointed judge believes God's will to be, regardless of the judged one's opinion, experience, or understanding. When we consider turning Jesus' second greatest commandment around to explore what it means to love ourselves, we recognize that we can find ourselves in the role of the self-appointed judge, judging not only others but ourselves. As we have well established, our goal for learning (or re-learning) to love ourselves must involve slowing down. We're not trying to determine God's will for all people; we're trying to learn the nuances of God's will in our own souls. When we discover that nuance, we encounter a certain freedom that comes from listening for the Spirit and discerning God's will for our lives, a freedom that enables us to trust that whatever God's will is, it is inherently good.

As an oldest child, I have a really hard time living into this whole "God's will" idea. In a culture of rugged individualism, as a hustler by nature and upbringing, as someone who has moved through life with a lot of survival mechanisms, letting go of my will is tough. I can talk the talk, but when it comes to actually surrendering to God's will—which inevitably means letting go of mine—I find it really hard.

A tool I have found helpful in my exploration of myself is the Enneagram. The Enneagram is a system that describes nine interconnected personality types, providing insights into a person's likely characteristics, inclinations, and relationships with others based on where they may identify themself within the system. I have identified myself as a Two on the Enneagram. Twos are known in the Enneagram world as "the Helpers." The core of the Enneagram is that we identify with a particular type because we recognize it as our go-to mode to feel safe in the world. Twos feel safest, most worthy of love when they are helping. Our hustle is helping. What's not to love about a helper? Yet one of the insights the Enneagram provides is an understanding of what a "healthy" type looks like versus an "unhealthy" type. When Twos are not healthy, our helping becomes more like controlling. I see this tendency in myself when I am out of balance.

As I was exploring the Enneagram, I listened to a podcast on understanding boundaries for Enneagram types. The woman speaking on the podcast identified as an Eight on the Enneagram. Eights are walking boundaries. They are a boundary. Their safety zone is within boundaries, and so they can create, maintain, and hold consequences for lack of boundaries with ease. It occurred to me that I didn't want to learn boundaries from an Eight, who likely had never struggled to set a boundary in their life. I needed to learn from another Two who had learned to set boundaries while shaking in her boots. Twos struggle with boundaries for lots of reasons, but mainly because if they are saying "no" to something or someone, it probably means they aren't helping, and that can be torturous for a Two. Can we feel safe in the world if we aren't helping?

I had a particularly large and cumbersome situation that I faced at one point, and my natural inclination was to do what I always do—help. But every angle I took to try to help, I encountered a roadblock. As I prayed about the situation, I kept hearing the Spirit whisper into my soul, "It's not your fight." What?! It so clearly appeared to be my fight. And while it made all kinds of good sense to help, I was also able to acknowledge loads of evidence that said otherwise as well. As I talked with people I trusted, I just kept clearly perceiving that in this incident I should NOT help. When I could get calm and quiet, which wasn't often during this time because my busy, anxious mind was constantly running and analyzing, I would hear the whispers of the Spirit again, "It's not your fight. Stand down."

A friend of mine said, "If it's not your fight, whose fight is it?"

When I took this to my spiritual director, I expected her to take the stance of my friend who had challenged me on whose fight it was. I expected her to say, "Caroline, of course this is your fight." But, she didn't. Rather she asked me about the God I believe in, the God in whom I put my faith and trust. I proceeded to tell her about the God of my understanding, the God of the Gospels who turns toward all of creation, who turns toward every human being in their suffering and in their joy. God is a God of compassion, kindness, and deep and abiding love; a God who yearns to care for us and live in union with us day in and day out; a God who wants nothing more than to *be with us*; a God whose son walked the earth to teach us how to love ourselves by receiving and trusting the deep and abiding love of God, and from that place how to genuinely love one another. This is a God whose benevolence is too big and wild for mere mortals to comprehend; a God whose grace is truly for all of creation, no picking and choosing; a God who has been with me in my darkest hours, my greatest joys, and all the mundane moments of life; a God whose Advocate, the Spirit, became a dear friend through my life and has guided me through wilderness and wonder.

She listened, nodding her head. Gentle smile, a grin on her kind face.

She encouraged me to be curious about what this God of my faith might be up to in asking me to trust that this situation wasn't my fight. How might God be taking care of me by asking me to "stand down"? Might God be encouraging me to feel safe in the world even without being "the helper" in every situation? Might some fights not be my fights because God has a different, better plan? Might taking on fights that aren't mine prevent the people genuinely called to the fight from claiming their space?

One of the easiest mistakes Twos can make is helping where they aren't being asked to help; "helping" when their help isn't actually useful or beneficial. When a Two's desire to help comes out of the need to feel safe in the world rather than truly wanting to provide needed support, then that person is not relying on a loving God. Humility is about staying rightsized with God. I remember who I am always in relationship to a loving God. I stay in my lane and allow God to be in charge of God's lane. Sometimes I get mixed up about the lanes. This situation taught me that some fights really aren't my fight. It showed me that I can genuinely feel safe in the world without taking on the fights God hasn't given me to fight. It taught me to ask God to strengthen my will to God's will. Rather than lean into my helper mode, I've had to learn to faithfully trust that I'm okay, I'm safe, even if I'm not helping.

The passage I started this chapter with from 2 Corinthians has nudged me into a new understanding and appreciation of flowing in God's will. Oftentimes, like most people, I cling to my own will out of a desire for control. Being in control helps me feel safe—I don't think that's particular to any Enneagram type, but rather just human nature. Yet what this reveals is that I naively believe that my will might somehow be better than God's. When I stop and challenge myself with that thought, I am able to see how ridiculous it is. Yet our subconscious mind often lingers in willfulness because following our own will satisfies our need for control. We forget to give control to God or are too nervous to do so. We cling to our own will because the alternative is scary.

This is complicated by the tendency of our society to tell us that a lack of willfulness is a weakness. Weakness isn't something most of us feel comfortable experiencing or admitting. Our culture encourages us to deny any weakness. Our wills must be strong, society says, and so we strengthen our will in order to defend our minds, hearts, and bodies. The more we sense and perceive our own weakness, the more robust and rigorous we push our will to become. In many ways, the creation and pursuit of our will is one of our greatest defense mechanisms. The places we care most deeply about are the places in our lives that we'd like to exert the most control over, so we exercise our will to maintain control, to influence them, and to make them "better."

Herein lies the divine invitation. Instead of pushing us to expand our will and exercise control over the things we worry about, the things we agonize over, the things we wish we had a lot more control of, God invites us to lean in to our weaknesses and bring these things to God. God invites us to trust the movement of the Spirit to meet us right in the middle of the very things we care most about and therefore would desire the most control over. When we turn to God instead of turning into ourselves for strength, the Spirit awakens within us a deep and abiding awareness that God's will is truly what is best for us and the people in our lives, and the Spirit inspires us to align our wants with God's wants. We then shift out of a perspective of contrast—God's will or our will. We lose our black and white thinking, and we allow the breath of the Spirit to yoke our will with the will of a loving God. Our will embraces the divine dance and allows God to lead.

Peter's Will Yoked with God's Will

The story of Peter in Acts 10-11 illustrates how we can align our will with God's will. In surrendering to this alignment of divine/human will, an opportunity breaks open to share grace with others in meaningful, life-giving ways. Peter experiences moment by moment divine intervention—a vision; hearing the divine voice not once, not twice, but three times; then the Spirit's instruction; hearing another speak of their experience with angels; and then experiencing the Holy Spirit falling upon them like a second Pentecost.

As we begin chapter 11, Jesus' followers are criticizing Peter for hanging out with those who don't belong in their circle: the Gentiles. We should immediately acknowledge some irony. Jesus was always hanging out with the "out" crowd, the people the "faithful" had determined to have fallen outside the circle of grace. The Pharisees complained against Jesus for this very thing and used it as an attempt to discredit him. Now Jesus' followers are lobbying the same criticism at Peter, which inspires him to explain to the criticizers step by step what has happened. He recounts the story that has just been told in the second half of chapter 10.

I love Peter's inclination to enlightening people's minds to the Spirit's wisdom. On Pentecost (Acts 2), when some believed that the faithful were drunk at nine in the morning, it was Peter who stood up and pulled the thread of wisdom from the prophet Joel through Jesus to the present moment, explaining the work of the Spirit. Here Peter cannot help but launch into a explanation of what is going on to try to help others see the movement of the Spirit.

First Peter was praying and, while in a prayerful realm, he saw a vision. It's a strange vision for sure—a large sheet is coming down from heaven, being lowered by its four corners. This image reminds me of playing with a parachute in gym class when I was in elementary school. The sheet comes close to Peter. As he looks at it closely, he sees four-footed animals, beasts of prey, reptiles, and birds of the air. And this voice says to him, "Get up, Peter; kill and eat" (Acts 10:13).

And, Peter says, "No way." He has spent his lifetime keeping strict dietary regulations as outlined in the Jewish faith. One bite, and there is no going back. He could no longer say nothing had ever entered his mouth after he took even one bite of something.

The divine voice comes a second time: "What God has made clean, you must not call profane." God is telling Peter ever so clearly that God is doing something new. God is enlightening Peter's mind. God is asking Peter to let go of old understandings and allow himself to risk God's grace being made ever wider. God is once again extending humanity's perception of the circle of grace. A third time the voice speaks. Then the vision ends.

At that very moment, three men appear. The Spirit herself tells Peter to go with them and instructs him to not make a distinction between the two groups of people. A few of Peter's friends go as well, and as they walk together, I can imagine Peter resisting the urge to think of these strangers as "them" and himself and followers of Jesus as "us." Eventually, they reach Cornelius's house and hear of Cornelius's experience with the Spirit.

Cornelius shares that he saw an angel standing in his home who told him to find Peter in Joppa, because Peter would give him a message that would save his whole family. Peter realizes that his experience and the experience of Cornelius are two puzzle pieces in the same divine narrative. God has enlightened both of their minds. Both have been given divine instruction to have this encounter with each other on behalf of the people they represent. God, the Holy Spirit, angels are all involved in orchestrating this experience between two people who will have a lasting impact on the entirety of the Christian faith.

As Peter retells this story to the people who had been criticizing him, Peter says, "And as I began to speak, the Holy Spirit fell upon them just as it had upon us at the beginning" (Acts 11:15). He remembers his own Pentecost experience from Acts 2, recalling the moment when the Holy Spirit filled all the believers and they spoke in different languages as the Spirit gave them ability. Here Peter once again witnessed the Holy Spirit fall upon the people before him, he tells the listeners. Peter recalls the words spoken by Jesus right before he ascended, "John baptized with water, but you will be baptized with the Holy Spirit" (Acts 11:16). He understands that what he witnessed was the Holy Spirit descending upon these people whom he would never have guessed God would speak to. He saw the Spirit invite them into the circle of grace and belonging. This is why he eats at the table with them. This is why he believes they have as much right to be within the circle of God's grace as anyone else.

The Holy Spirit has clearly enlightened Peter's mind and stirred his heart. Peter put the pieces together and saw the revelation—God has given the Gentiles the same gift as has been given to the Jewish people. Just as the Spirit prompted him to acknowledge, there is no *them* and *us*. We are all God's people. We are all hungry to connect with a loving God and live in healthy, life-giving, joyful connection to one another.

Peter's recounting of his experience causes everyone present to fall silent. They get it. In the silence, the Spirit is moving through them, enlightening their minds and stirring their hearts in a new way. They take in this new message, allowing God's revelation to change the very orientation as to how they have perceived and experienced God's love and sense of belonging for themselves and others. The Holy Spirit is erasing any demarcation of *them* and *us*. They understand that we are all people hungry to connect with a loving God and live in healthy, life-giving, joyful connection to one another.

What is fascinating to me is that God was asking Peter to break what he had always understood God's rules to be in the first place. Peter did not eat certain types of meat because he understood from Jewish law that was the rule. When he hears God's voice asking him to go against God's own law, he must have been confused at best. Perhaps that is why it took God repeating this new message three times. Peter had to trust God's will so much that he was willing to break a law of God's so that God could do something new with God's people.

The stirring of the heart and the enlightenment of the mind can only go so far if we are unwilling to be strengthened by God's will to act on that stirring and enlightenment. People can open their hearts and minds without ever changing their behavior and attitudes. When we allow the Spirit to breathe through us and strengthen God's will within us, we can courageously use that stirring and enlightening to extend grace to ourselves and to others.

When a whole band of people criticize you, it can be arduous to step out in faith and act in accordance with the stirring of your heart and enlightenment of your mind. By way of the Spirit, God gives us both clarity and strength to carry forward with whatever

God gives us to do. I so appreciate Peter's words when he says to those listening, "Who was I that I could hinder God?" This is the key conclusion to the experience. Enlightening, stirring, and strengthening open us to the realization that if we do not step out in faith and extend grace, we will be hindering God. When Peter asks this question, my own soul is prompted to wonder, "How am I hindering God?" and "Who am I to hinder God?" The question causes us to realize that we have the power to hinder God—that says something about the power of our will. Part of our work is to sense when our actions or inactions, words or lack of words, are hindering God. Most of the ways I hinder God usually live in my blind spots, which is one of the many reasons I continue in relationship with spiritual companions, friends, *anam caras*, therapy, and other avenues that help me see beyond myself.

God's will is not a path that simply seeks to allow God to be in control of us and the world. God's will provides for our betterment, as well as for the betterment our neighbors. When God strengthens us to yoke our will with God's will, what follows is the receiving and giving of grace. We can think of God's will as harsh and meant to punish us or make life more difficult or painful, but we must check that theology. Is that the God we believe in? It amazes me how often I can believe and profess in a loving God and then resist God's will because I think it will hurt me or someone I love. I don't believe in a punishing, harsh God, yet when it comes to following God's will, I have to question my lived theology, the way my beliefs about God manifest in the actions I take. If I believe in a loving God, then I can trust that God's will is the path to wholeness for everyone involved.

When Peter shares his experience with the criticizers, they experience their own awakening, and, in doing so, something shifts within them. Peter's words allow the Spirit to create an enlightenment of their minds and a stirring of their hearts. With this shift in perspective, what they once were criticizing Peter for is now a cause for rejoicing. They say to one another, "Then God has given even to the Gentiles the repentance that leads to life" (Acts 11:18). They receive not only a stirring of their hearts and an enlightenment of their minds, but are empowered in the Spirit's strength to move from criticism to joyful celebration. It takes a certain amount of strength to change their actions, to widen the circle, to let God's grace move in the world..

Widening the circle of grace will always take a certain amount of courage. We tend to react to extensions of grace with fear, as if there is room only for a few. If we allow people into the circle of grace, we worry, then maybe we're jeopardizing our place within the circle. Yet God is constantly showing us through the scriptures—and hopefully through our own lived experience—that there is room for everyone. The core of God's will is always grace, which means no one is left out.

INVITATION TO PRACTICE: ACKNOWLEDGING OUR WILL & BEING CURIOUS ABOUT GOD'S WILL

Sit quietly, allowing your body and mind to find some stillness. Anchor your attention in your breath. After a few moments of gentle breathing and settling, allow yourself to be curious about your own willfulness. What aspects of your life are you most prone to experience surges of your own willfulness? What is underneath the willfulness—fear, trepidation, desire, shame? Allow God to see your will and whatever drives it. You might imagine God holding all of it in pure light. Be curious about God's compassion for your will. How might God ease and heal whatever drives your will? In that ease and healing, be curious how God might yoke your will to God's will, which is full of love, goodness, health, and wellbeing. When you're ready to conclude this practice, end with this prayer or with one of your own.

Holy and gracious God, help me to know your will deep in my bones and not be afraid of it. May your Spirit assist me when my own will gets spicy, out of hand, and actually works against me. May your Spirit ever so gentle yoke my will with yours so that I may live in the goodness of your love, health , and wellbeing not only for my sake but also for those all around me. Amen.

CHAPTER TEN

Resurrected Living: Living Unbound in the Spirit

The fruit of the Spirit is love, joy, peace, patience, kindness, generosity, faithfulness, gentleness, and self-control. There is no law against such things.

GALATIANS 5:22-23

God with Us

As we have seen, living embodied grace is about breathing with the Spirit, embodying God's love, and allowing God to enlighten our mind, stir our heart, and strengthen our will. But living an embodied life is also a letting-go process. It's letting go of all the things that bind us, all the things that get in the way of allowing ourselves to be breathed, enlightened, stirred, strengthened. Living embodied grace is ultimately living a life unbound, so as to be free to live within the breath of the Spirit and embody the love of God with abundance.

Let's return to Mary kneeling at the feet of Jesus after her brother Lazarus has died. Mary runs to Jesus and says to him, "Lord, if you had been here, my brother would not have died." She is weeping at his feet. The scripture says, "When Jesus saw her weeping, and the Jews who came with her also weeping, he was greatly disturbed in spirit and deeply moved." Three sentences later, scripture reads, "Jesus began to weep."

There are many places within the Gospels where Jesus turns toward those who are suffering. He engages them, speaks to them, and heals many of them. This is the only place in the Gospels, however, where it says that Jesus was *greatly disturbed in spirit and deeply moved*. It's the only place in the text that says *Jesus began to weep*. We see here the depth of Jesus' compassion and empathy, his willingness and ability to be moved by human suffering. He is modeling the essence of living embodied love. Because of how it is written, it appears that Jesus was both moved by his friend Mary's tears and also by the tears of the grieving community as well. He had come to know and therefore love and care for these people, and in their pain and suffering, he felt with them. You might even say that their weeping and grief broke open something in Jesus that allowed his feelings to flow forth as well.

How often we forget that Emmanuel—"God with us"—is an actual being with us in our pain and suffering? I have heard so many people over the years talk about God being with them, but there was still a sense of distance to God's presence. There was no up close, empathic, compassionate, divine presence with them or within them in their tears and pain. There was no loving divine presence that was *greatly disturbed in spirit and deeply moved.* No divine presence *weeping* with them.

Being broken open by the pain and suffering of life are often our most vulnerable experiences. The moments when our emotions are flowing, or raging, are often the moments when we are most in need of God's loving and compassionate presence. In these moments, we need a God who is right there with us, offering to be so close to our pain and vulnerability that God experiences that pain and vulnerability too. We need a loving God whose presence feels imminent, palpable, tangible in some way. We need God's love made manifest in the depths of our soul so that our skin is blessed by that loving presence.

From the human perspective of Mary and the grieving community, Jesus is late. Once physically there, however, he embodies an immense ability to be with them in their pain. This is the Jesus we have come to know through the Gospels: God's presence truly being with those in pain and suffering, turning toward and being with those whom society has written off and left behind. The ways in which Jesus turns toward the suffering offers us a role model to turn not only toward others' suffering, but also to turn toward our own suffering and allow Jesus to be with us in our pain.

One of the parts that is so moving is that it's not just about Jesus being present to others' pain. Jesus is also broken open. His emotions are stirred, and his tears flow. This is a whole new level and depth to Jesus being Emmanuel, God with us. He isn't merely a stoic, emotionally static presence; he has entered the emotional messiness of the human experience with Mary and the grieving community. He feels their pain, is greatly disturbed in spirit, and deeply moved. This is a divine presence that is close, intimate, and engaged. Like a loving parent that feels with their child when life is messy, unfair, and painful.

Jesus models for us how we are broken open in life by our own pain and suffering. Jesus allows himself to be moved by Mary, the grieving community, and his own pain about his friend Lazarus. Though Jesus knows he will soon raise Lazarus from the dead, he also knows that the human experience of dying is difficult, painful, and scary.

Some in the crowd experience Jesus' tears as evidence for how deeply he cared about Lazarus. Others are still so angry with him for not preventing Lazarus' death that they cannot see or are unwilling to be moved by Jesus' experience. You know, Jesus could have thrown up his arms and said, "Enough with you doubters and haters. I clearly cannot get through to you all. I'm out of here." But he doesn't. Jesus moves to the tomb.

Even though Martha is worried about rolling back the stone due to the awful stench that will soon pierce their senses, Jesus tells them to remove the stone. He makes it clear to everyone by speaking to God aloud in their presence that what is to happen next is to create belief in God who sent him. Jesus cries, "Lazarus, come out!" and Lazarus walks out of the tomb. His hands and feet are still bound with the burial cloths. His face is still covered with the cloths his sisters gently wrapped him in for burial. Jesus says to them, "Unbind him, and let him go."

Being Unbound

Over the last couple years, I have been so moved by the particulars of this story's ending, details I never really paid attention to before. Jesus so easily could have walked over to Lazarus and unbound him, or the movement of the Holy Spirit could have released the bindings from Lazarus as he walked out of the tomb. Jesus instead chose to involve the grieving community in the resurrection experience. He required their participation in the unbinding of their beloved family member, friend, and neighbor. Lazarus' community becomes part of what sets him free to live again.

No one lives into a resurrected life alone. We're social creatures by design. We need each other. We are part of what sets each other free. It can be tempting to run back to the old way of life prior to our death experiences. It can be easy to want to cling to old habits and old ways even once the binding is removed. It's part of why we need each other so much. Lazarus didn't walk out of the tomb, become unbound by his friends and family, and go on to live a perfect life—there is no such thing as a perfect life. I imagine his strength had to rebuild after the tomb. I imagine he had to mentally and emotionally process the event for some time. He must have needed to go over it repeatedly with his sisters, Jesus, and his neighbors. I wonder whether Lazarus embraced his resurrected life completely, with relative ease, or if he struggled to live into the meaning of it. How much work did it take for him to integrate his new life with his former?

The curious thing about being set free is that it is a holy act of transformation. The point is not to eventually get all the pieces to fit back together again like Humpty Dumpty. When we are unbound by the Spirit in community, our lives are changed forever. Initially, we might fight like crazy to stitch it all back together again, trying like mad to make our lives look and feel like they once did. But we cannot go back to our previous way of being. In fact, our very human natural instincts to put ourselves all back together again in the old way works against the movement of God. God doesn't unbind us purely for the experience of being unbound. God sets us free to have that experience and then every experience after as well. Transformation happens in the being unbound, but the transformation doesn't end after the unbinding is complete. We continue to be transformed. In transformation, we drop down into the essence of our being and are better able to live from the God-woven core of our being. I've always thought of transformation as returning home to the wholeness of God within us rather than being made new. That return to the inherent wholeness within us *is* something being made new. Most of us lead very fractured lives, so when we have moments of integrated wholeness, it is transformation. Every time we return home to God's wholeness within us, we are being made new in the experience of wholeness.

The reality for many of us is that becoming unbound is more of a process than a light switch. Being unbound may feel like true freedom—freedom to experience life fully from the depth of God's goodness within us. But sometimes we might feel like we are still bound in what held us back before. We may feel one day as if we are in the flow of the Spirit, aware of a palpable sense of being unbound by grief, mental challenges, a raging emotional heart, troubling thought patterns, and then we wake up the next day missing all of that sense of freedom. Rarely have I found that being unbound is a linear process. Though it can happen in a moment, most of us move through a non-linear pattern of highs and lows, much like every other human experience. Do not despair. As we become unbound, we find ourselves more and more able to simply breathe with the Spirit moment by moment and stay in her flow. The practices we establish help us find this flow, this freedom, more and more often, and help us live more of our life unbound than bound.

As we start to experience this freedom of the Spirit more often, we can start to feel unmoored from our previous life. Freedom is glorious, but, by nature, it comes without many restraints. What happens when we are set free from what binds us—what takes the place of the energy and effort it took to live within those bindings? Freedom in the Spirit takes many forms, and it is a process to rebuild a new life unbound in the Spirit to take the place of the old. When we walk away from the toxic relationship, we must not fill that space with another toxic relationship. When we embrace the trial of living through an illness—or accept the dying process—we cannot replace the energy we spent on fear with fear of something else. What comes next when we leave a destructive job? What happens when the negative emotions and cycles begin to fade? How do we move through our days with more calm and ease than chaos and anxiety? What do we lean into when we're no longer consumed with what has bound our hearts, minds, and lives? What happens once we are unbound?

Resurrected Living

As I allow myself to be unbound by the Spirit in community, the natural place to lean into is an embodiment of God's love in mind, body, and spirit. Evidence of transformation becomes the model for how we engage ourselves, the people around us, the world. When we are unbound, we discover a natural desire to *be* God's love in the world and to share that love with others. To me, this most commonly looks and feels like an organic outflow of the fruit of the Spirit.

It is my deep and abiding belief that we are made of the gifts of the Spirit. As the old parts of us are shed through the unbinding process, we find room to align ourselves with the goodness that is already woven within us. We don't have to go out looking for them. In our creation, God weaves love, joy, peace, patience, kindness, generosity, faithfulness, gentleness and self-control (or what I like to call equanimity) within every fiber and cell of our being. God's goodness is the essence of our being.

The more I live into the definition of grace and allow the Spirit to flow through me, the more the fruit of the Spirit simply becomes a natural outpouring from my being. I've watched this with other people too. Simple occurrences that might go unnoticed suddenly become a resonance of the inner goodness. It's important to note that when Paul talks of the fruit of the Spirit in Galatians chapter 5, he speaks of them collectively, which indicates that, unlike the differing gifts the Spirit gives, the fruit of the Spirit are inclusive—we have and can exhibit all of them. Though these fruits sound simple enough, as we move through a discussion of each, we'll find there can be complexity in the embodiment of God's wholeness. Each moment offers us an invitation to both lean into any given fruit manifesting within us with the help of our loving God and to be guided by the breath of the Spirit.

Love

The first fruit naturally is love. Love is the cornerstone of the Gospels, the essence of the being of Jesus and his message of good news. As this book has woven together, hopefully there is a growing awareness that love is also the cornerstone of our lives. We are made in God's love. Love is our spiritual DNA. Love is our spiritual birthright. We are made in love, recipients of love, worthy of love, and bearers of love. Living embodied grace requires us to not only know this love intellectually, it also requires us to claim this love in our bones so much so that love radiates from our beings.

My experience of God's love is that it is woven into every fiber and cell of our beings. And, in our forgetful humanity (because life can frankly be so hard!), we are constant recipients of God's love. God is constantly replenishing God's love within us. As we discussed earlier in the book, one of the great resources of centering prayer and meditation is the opportunity to very intentionally return to God's love within us over and over again.

We can allow this formal practice to guide and influence our informal practice of life. As we move about our daily rhythm of life, we can remember both that we are deeply loved by God and that we are bearers of God love in the world. When we claim the love woven deep within our bones, we realize we have a divine source of love to share with others.

Love is a powerful force, but we use the word for such a variety of experiences and relationships. We use the same word "love" for the pizza we just ate as we do for our beloved deceased grandmother. This can be troubling, because obviously there is a different kind of love for pizza than for beloved grandmothers. It can cause us to think that true love has to be grand. But this is not true. We can actually recognize an invitation in our excessive use of the word *love*. What if every time we used the word "love" (whether for our favorite food or a beloved family member), we really let ourselves feel that love? What if we took the opportunity to connect with what it feels like to be deeply grateful for something to the point of loving it?

As an Enneagram Two, I have a hypersensitivity to loving conditions, to what qualifies as love and what doesn't. Perhaps especially because I'm a Two, grounding in God's love has been invaluable to every relationship I have had, whether personally or professionally. Receiving God's love, loving myself, and allowing God's love to flow through me towards others has been a game changer. I often think that if an Enneagram Two can learn how to receive and share God's love, anyone can. This is such a daunting task for most Twos because we have a tendency to hustle for love most of our lives instead of simply receiving it. Most Twos try to self-generate love to offer others rather than going through the vulnerable process of being transformed by God's love and sharing God's love with others. It's my sense that most Twos find it very difficult to accept God's love because deep down they don't feel worthy of it.

Take an honest look into your own relationship with love. Do you claim your belovedness in a loving God? If not, what gets in the way? Be honest about who you love and how you love. Do you love from a place of sharing God's love with others? Do you love from a place of "should"? ("I should love this person because they love me.") Do you love from a place of "have to"? ("I have to love them; they are my family.") Or do you allow yourself to be filled up with God's love so that the excess of that divine love overflows into your relationships with others? How do you know when you're hustling for love verses sharing the love of God with someone else? How do you maintain some semblance of balance within your life of both receiving God's love and allowing God's love to flow from you?

Joy

Sometimes I wonder if God doesn't have better things to do than tend to my joy. I've heard numerous other people ponder the same. "Does God really care about my joy? Aren't there bigger things for God to be about than anyone's joy?" In chapter 15 of the Gospel of John, Jesus tells his disciples he is the true vine and God is the vinegrower. Jesus uses this metaphor to teach that when we follow the wisdom God has provided us, we are abiding in God's love and God's love abides in us. When the love of God is flowing, we are able to bear fruit and, in doing so, become disciples of a loving God. He speaks of the love, the commitment, the relationship that grows between the vinegrower, the vine, and the branches. Then at the end of this metaphor, Jesus says, "I have said these things to you so that my joy may be in you, and that your joy may be complete." Jesus is pulling the thread of wisdom through the good news. When we live the first fruit of love, it paves the way for us to experience joy. Our abiding in God's love matters to God, and the first fruit of love plants the seeds to experience joy within the garden of our lives.

We often are of the mindset that joy is a quality we have to go out and find. We rarely expect joy to find us, much less bubble up organically from within. Yet when I stay aligned with the Spirit, I do notice that joy tends to find me in the most unexpected and ordinary ways.

I have never been a fan of Halloween, so much so that at times I feel like a Halloween Grinch. Outside of the few years when my boys were little and enjoyed picking out costumes, I have always wanted to skip right over this holiday. I felt this way until a real live butterfly appeared one Halloween. I love butterflies, and I had decided to dress up as a butterfly for Halloween this particular year at work. I was getting ready to process in for our All Hallow's Eve worship service, dressed in my butterfly wings, when a little butterfly appeared at the back of the church. She happened to be Dorothy, the daughter of my dear friend Carrie. Here was Dorothy in butterfly wings and a butterfly mask around her eyes. It's like the Spirit had whispered to both of us, *wear wings today!* I was flooded with joy seeing this little butterfly. I asked her if she'd like to process with me and sit up front for the service. She was delighted to float down the aisle; she leaned in like she was made for this moment and had been waiting for it to manifest. She even came forward with me when it was time for the homily. We spread our wings, and I talked about the delight of flying in our dreams. As if this joy wasn't enough, the next morning Carrie texted to say that Dorothy had flown in her dreams that night.

I adore when the Spirit weaves her precious presence into our daily and nightly lives and reminds us through ordinary occurrences that joy abounds. We can delight in each other and the synchronicities of life. She can even breathe under our wings and make us fly in our dreams. Maybe God is trying to make his joy complete in us, and maybe it's not all that complex. When we have an open heart, we can be ready to welcome whatever delight the Spirit wants to deliver.

Peace

Everyone seems to want more peace. We want more calm in our minds and ease in bodies. We seek a balm for our soul. We want to know peace, and we want to know it intimately. When resurrected Jesus appears to the disciples in the Upper Room, the first words out of his lips are "Peace be with you." According to the Gospel of John, he even says them again almost within the same breath. It seems natural that Jesus would say these words; the disciples are likely going to be startled at the least, more likely terrified, at seeing Jesus after they knew him to be dead. Starting off with words to sooth the nervous system is a good idea, yet I wonder if there isn't something more here. Perhaps Jesus is extending a blessing, an instruction on a way of being in post-resurrected life. Now that Jesus has faced and overcome death, maybe the ability to live in peace each and every day of life is his gift to the disciples and to us.

I have wondered how my days might flow differently if I were to start by saying to myself, "Peace be with you this day." Through this statement, I remind myself that God journeys alongside me to help me maintain the peace with which I was created. Each encounter I have provides the opportunity to remember this peace. Before I open my mouth, I can take a split second to recognize the opportunity I have to extend peace to whomever I am talking to. My awareness of this allows the possibility for peace to flow between us.

When we live connected to our inherent peace, the peace woven into and through our bodies by a loving God in our creation, we move about the world differently. We're more likely to respond rather than react both to our ourselves and our neighbors. In many ways, starting every interaction from a place of peace opens us to share and embody the other fruit of the Spirit with more ease and strength as well. If we're feeling peaceful, we're more likely to treat our partner, child, or co-worker with patience, kindness, and generosity. If we're hyped up on stress and cannot access any peace in our mind, body or spirit, we struggle to engage ourselves or others with patience, kindness, and generosity. Staying tapped into the divine peace within creates fertile ground for the rest of the fruit of the Spirit to flourish.

Patience

Living in a world that seems to move faster as technology speeds us along makes patience an increasingly difficult quality to come by. Yet engaging a little patience can go a long way to creating healthy change in this world. Consider patience with yourself. How might your days improve if you were able to draw from an inner source of patience with yourself?

Throughout the Gospels, we experience Jesus as a patient presence with those he encounters. There are several places during his exchanges with others where it seems he's going to lose his patience and snap. When the disciples aren't comprehending what he's saying—especially when they seemingly understood a few days ago—or when the Pharisees are resistant to and threatened by Jesus' wisdom, he always maintains his patient presence. A reoccurring example of this is when Jesus heals on the Sabbath, effectively breaking the rule that one doesn't work on the Sabbath. Each time, the Pharisees try to trap him in his disobedience to the law, but Jesus never lets their words or actions affect his decisions. Maybe Jesus never felt bothered or reactive about their attempts to trap him. Whatever the case, I imagine Jesus facing those who challenged him, taking a big breath, and dropping down into the deep well of patience within before responding.

When I can stay grounded in the first three fruits (love, joy and peace), patience is infinitely easier to imbue. When I'm running low on love for myself and others, when joy has fallen by the wayside, when the peace that surpasses all understanding has passed me by, patience is usually out of the question for me. Raising children has been a daily pull for patience for me, especially raising teenagers. Many days, I wonder if I'll ever know the fruit of patience again! When I can take some deep breaths, slow myself down, and tap into the vast love, joy, and peace I have experienced in my children, I can more easily tap into the patience that is patiently waiting for me.

Lately, I've also noticed how much ease it brings me when people are patient with me. I have a wonderful supervisor, Bonnie. Sometimes I don't get things to her on time, or I overlook details, and even so, she's patient. She doesn't sweat the small stuff. She rolls with it. Her ability to not get flustered offers me room to stay at ease rather than shift into a place of tension. Her palpable embodiment of patience is such a gift to me, reminding me of why I want to practice the fruit of patience in my own life. Lack of patience so easily leads to breakdowns in communication and relationships. Patience keeps things open and fluid. The embodiment of patience for oneself and for others allows the other fruits to keep growing and flowing. Without patience, it's hard to stay open to love, joy, and peace. Without patience, it's also incredibly difficult to lean into kindness.

Kindness

Over the years when I've talked to my children about our family values, kindness is always at the top. Perhaps it's because I have known great unkindness in my life, or maybe I simply like the way it feels to be kind to someone else. I do know that when I am the recipient of someone else's kindness, I can more easily access all the gifts within me, including my own kindness.

In many ways, as I read the Gospels what I see and hear Jesus doing and saying is a mediation of loving-kindness. Jesus is the embodiment of all the fruit of the Spirit—he serves as a great example of what the fruits look and sound like in human form. And he tends to lead with loving kindness as he encounters people, especially those who need healing and those who have been marginalized. Even when he's challenging someone's behavior or attempting to show a different way, he does so with an undercurrent of kindness. He speaks from the deep well of kindness within him so that the content he shares is delivered with immense love. What might it be like to approach ourselves—especially the parts of ourselves we don't like—with loving-kindness? What if we turn towards these troublesome parts of ourselves as Jesus did and offer them loving-kindness?

For a period of time in my life, I suffered from night terrors. I would wake up in the middle of the night with a pounding heart, anxiety racing through my veins, and sweat drenching my pajamas. All I desperately wanted was to sleep in peace. Over time, I learned to turn towards this physical and mental pain with inner compassion and kindness. I could be gentle, patient, loving, and kind toward myself and the anxiety that flooded my system. In all honesty, in my fatigue, I rarely could remember to call upon Jesus' loving-kindness in those moments. Yet, learning to embody a deep sense of loving-kindness for myself, regardless of whether I could access God's love directly in that moment or not, allowed me to approach the situation differently. I learned from a loving God how to be loving toward myself, how to be kind, and then how to embody that loving kindness for others as the need arises.

Generosity

The fruit of generosity has become somewhat difficult to imbue in Western society. Our capitalist, consumer culture encourages us to place the focus on what we can get for ourselves, not on what we can offer to others. Even as Christians, we struggle to understand just what scripture means by generosity. We often confuse generosity and the prosperity gospel, yet the fruit of generosity is not the same as God being generous with us so that we prosper in specific and measurable ways. Our loving God is generous with us human beings in so many ways. It becomes part of our discipleship—how we live in response to God's grace—to offer generosity to others. The fruit of generosity is less about measurables and more about an orientation. Are we generous in our interpretations of other people's behavior and ideas? Are we generous with the ways we think and act towards ourselves?

For a long time, I've found myself curious about what it means to embody a spirit of generosity toward myself and other people. Offering a spirit of generosity to others has always come far easier for me than extending a spirit of generosity to myself. I've had to learn from the Spirit, following her guidance to broaden my ability to practice generosity with myself. At the same time, I have had to learn to dial back my generosity with others because it proved to be harmful to me. Learning to be generous is a balance: sometimes when we're too generous with others, the lack of accountability ends up causing more harm than good, often to everyone involved. Embodying all of the fruit of the Spirit requires us to seek the guidance of the Spirit in how much or little of a particular fruit is called for any given situation at any given time. We've been taught—directly or indirectly, consciously or subconsciously—to give everything we have. Yet as I have grown in my faith and wisdom, I understand that I need to be fed too. We can allow the Spirit to guide us into a life of balance that is generous towards ourselves so that we stay healthy, strong, and capable of bearing good fruit while also being generous with others.

Faithfulness

I so often think about faithfulness as showing up. We show up to our relationships to God, self, and others in faithfulness. Whether we're showing up in prayer, meditation, reading of scripture, attuning to the breath of the Spirit, or discerning what to do next based on our covenant with a loving God, all of these are practices and acts of faithfulness. The ways we show up for ourselves and others is also how we enliven the fruit of faithfulness.

I also come home to faithfulness being a two-way street. It's not only about our faithfulness to God, it's also about God's faithfulness to and with us. Throughout the gospels, we learn of a loving God who shows up for his people through his Son. We hear of the Spirit's guidance, the voice of angels, and witness Jesus' own words and actions. Part of what builds our capacity to be faithful to God, ourselves, and one another is learning from and trusting God's faithfulness with us.

Naturally, we grow our capacity to be faithful with one another through building trust. Consciously or subconsciously, we want the other party to "go first." I'll be faithful if you will. Being faithful can sometimes feel vulnerable and risky. Will the other person be faithful too? Will they show up in wholeness not only wanting what is best for themselves but also wanting what is best for me?

I wrote a children's book about the fruit of the Spirit called *Spirit Fruit*. I explained the fruit of faithfulness as the fruit that is needed for the times that we don't want to be the fruit of the Spirit—because we're tired or mad or upset or reactive. In those moments when we dig down deep and choose to embody the fruits with God's help anyway, we are embodying the fruit of faithfulness. Faithfulness has an element of intentionality and integrity. Faithfulness is about standing with the core of our being where the Spirit resides within us and being willing to be and act from this core stance.

In the story of the prodigal pon (Luke 15:11-32), the older son is resentful when it comes to his faithfulness. He has stayed with his father and worked faithfully by his side, while his younger brother went off and squandered his inheritance. Yet when the little brother comes home and is shown great love and grace by their father, the older brother refuses to celebrate his brother's return. Perhaps he never realized that his faithfulness had strings attached. Can we be faithful even at times that we cannot show love, joy, peace, patience, kindness, and generosity to others? Can I be faithful and withhold all the fruits? In all the cases in my own life, when I thought I was being faithful and yet simultaneously withheld the fruits of the Spirit in my actions toward others, it was a massive opportunity to wrestle it out with God.

Gentleness

The Spirit's gift of gentleness has always made me think of the dove gently floating down from heaven to hover over Jesus as he is being baptized by John the Baptist in the Jordan River—that is until I was teaching an adult education class on the Holy Spirit. As we discussed Jesus being baptized, someone in the class commented that the experience must have been overwhelming to all the bystanders. He said that it must have been unexpected and radical for all of these people going to the Jordan to be baptized by John, not anticipating the skies to open, a dove to appear, and the voice of God to boom from the heavens. He read this part of scripture as anything but gentle, saying it felt more like God hitting the bystanders over the head with a two-by-four. I love how two people can read the same thing in scripture and experience such different things, seeing God, Jesus, and the Spirit in such a different light.

The fruits of the Spirit build on one another, so that by the time we turn to discuss gentleness, we find a lot of the same ideas that we've already discussed. As with patience, kindness, and generosity, we must learn to be gentle with ourselves and with others. Many of us have learned to be hard on ourselves in order to succeed in life. We can be hard drivers and relentless self-critics, which doesn't leave much room for gentleness. The harder we are on ourselves, the harder we tend to be on others, sometimes without even knowing it. Paying attention to the gift of gentleness asks us to pay attention to how we talk to ourselves and one another. It offers the opportunity to question and reflect on the validity of our inner critic, whether directed at ourselves or others. Is there an element of God's gentleness within our being and in our approach to others?

As with the other fruits, we must be discerning and listen for the Spirit's guidance on when and how to embody the fruits of the Spirit. Tough love is sometimes necessary, and it likely doesn't feel gentle. Embodying the fruit of the spirit doesn't ask us to be doormats, allowing others to walk all over us as we show love and gentleness. Toughness and gentleness are not necessarily opposing forces: there are times that tough is the very thing called for, and toughness can be simultaneously embodied with all the fruits, including gentleness. It is the manner in which we act that matters. I can be tough in a boundary and engage myself and the other person with firm gentleness in setting and maintaining that boundary.

Self-Control/Equanimity

During the COVID-19 pandemic, as the global anxiety statistics were rising for all ages, I found myself curious in new ways about the fruit of self-control. I've come to see this gift linked with the ability and willingness to be faithful. Can I act out of a place of wholeness that reflects all the fruits of the Spirit? This usually requires some self-control.

I also have a great curiosity about how self-control is about the equanimity that the meditation world speaks of and practices. When I was training to be a Mindfulness-Based Stress Reduction (MBSR) teacher, the word "equanimity" kept appearing. Maybe I just noticed it appear because it had something to teach me. In any case, equanimity is this state of being that remains neutral or keeps returning to neutral, presumably with some ease. I've learned over time it isn't a static state. Equanimity is more like a constant realignment with our center, so that we're not becoming reactive and thrown from this core. For me, self-control and equanimity have become a great deal about self-regulation of emotions, thoughts, words, and behaviors. I used to naively think that most adults walked around with self-control, an understanding that does not bear out in reality. As it turns out, self-control is fairly difficult and rather rare. It can feel like a full-time job some days to regulate our nervous system, thought processes, and emotions. All of us can benefit greatly from learning how to self-regulate. Mindfulness, meditation, prayer, breath work, and a host of other spiritual practices can assist us in harnessing self-control and equanimity.

To be human is to be reactive at times. It's helpful to be aware of what triggers us and what our reactivity feels like in our bodies, minds, and hearts. When we know what throws us out of control, we can better work with our emotions to regain self-control again. When we are aware of what we feel like when we move into dysregulation, we have an easier time using practices that align us again. Through practice, I have become very aware that when I am dysregulated, I have lost my alignment with the breath of the Spirit. When my equanimity is off, I have a very difficult time tapping into and living out the Spirit's fruit. Through more practice, I now understand what helps me realign with the Spirit. Even something as simple as slowing my breathing down and intentionally breathing with the Spirit for a few breaths can be enough to help me find my equanimity again. Asking for the Spirit's help and opening to her love, peace, patience, kindness, generosity, and gentleness assist in regaining self-control.

Holy Anger

The fruits make the Spirit sound gentle. Let us be clear: the Spirit is not always gentle. Sometimes her holy breath comes more like a roar, igniting within us holy anger. The older I get, the longer I live, the more I believe that anger is truly holy. Anger can be an indication of the Spirit signaling injustice, calling for a need for change, or teaching us about a grief that needs to be expressed and processed. When taken as a pure, raw emotion, anger tells us when a line has been crossed. Anger throws a red flag in the air that says, "Warning! Warning!" Anger gets such a bad rap because we often react too quickly to our anger, instead of allowing ourselves to feel our anger, sit with it, and let it run through us before we act on what needs to be addressed. Many of us get immediately activated by our anger and lash out at ourselves or other people, making the situation worse. If we don't learn to listen to our anger and find constructive ways to work with it and respond to it, anger can become toxic and dangerous. The emotion itself, however, is valuable. Anger can be sacred.

Embodied Fruits

When Paul lists the fruits of the Spirit, he follows it up by saying "There is no law against such things" (Gal. 5:23). It seems pretty obvious that there is no law against such things as faithfulness, love, joy, and peace. Yet just because there isn't a law against them doesn't mean they are always easy to understand in any given moment nor easy to embody. Again, for me the trick has been taking the time to discern with God and wise companions (friends, mentors, spiritual companions, *anam caras,* and therapists) what the will of God might be, so that by God's help I can lean into faithfulness and embody what God has given me to do and/or be.

With our minds enlightened, our hearts stirred, and our wills strengthened, everyday life becomes a source of the fruit of the Spirit. When I meditate on the fruits of the Spirit, I understand better that we are made of these fruits. The core of our being is love, joy, peace, patience, kindness, generosity, faithfulness, gentleness, and equanimity. The essence of our DNA is this nine-fold goodness. However, the stress and trauma of life pile up and make it harder for us to access this inner Spirit goodness.

Years ago, when life was simpler and my pace of life was slower, the natural flow of life made it easier to sluff off or process the wear and tear, the traumas of life. We live in such fast-paced times with such rapid-fire stimulation coming at us constantly, we don't make much space or have much bandwidth to shed the things that challenge us, leaving us increasingly detached from the essence of who we really are.

We aren't expected to perfectly embody the Spirit's gifts each day. The gifts are a way of life that we strive for. The Spirit's gifts are woven within us in our creation, and by the constant tether to the Spirit and her breath, we embody them and offer them to ourselves and the world around us. Living embodied grace is not only essential for our connection to a loving God, our own souls, and the breath of the Spirit. It is imperative for how we're called to be in the world. When we can allow ourselves to be the fruits of the Spirit guided by the breath of the Spirit, loving our neighbors isn't such a big deal. Loving our neighbors simply becomes an organic flow from our inner God-given wholeness.

My prayer is that in reading this book you find yourself a bit more encouraged and grounded in the essence of your being—the love God wove within you in addition to the love that God continues to pour through you. I hope your connection to this very real divine love assists you in loving yourself with more ease and commitment. May we all have the courage to drop the hustle, draw ourselves within the circle of grace God has already placed us within, and see and love others from this place of interconnected grace. In this way of loving ourselves and one another as God loves us, may we be the beacon of light for which the world is hungry.

INVITATION TO PRACTICE: RESURRECTED LIVING

Sit quietly, allowing your body and mind to find some stillness, and anchor your attention in your breath. Notice any organic invitation from your body to slow your breathing down. Elongate your inbreath and outbreath. As you open your awareness to breathe with the Spirit, notice any ease, calm, peace in your body, or any feelings and sensations that indicate you are in the flow of the Spirit. Gently allow yourself to notice anything that is binding you in this moment, whether it be a thought, a story you're telling yourself, a strong emotion, or a physical pain. Allow the Spirit to breathe through that binding, and imagine the Spirit gently releasing the binding.

As you experience the binding easing from your mind, heart and body, allow yourself to come back into that flow of the Spirit. Notice if it's easier to access the fruits of the Spirit within you—love, joy, peace, patience, kindness, generosity, faithfulness, gentleness, and self-control/equanimity. Give yourself some time to breathe with these fruits. Notice where you experience them in your body. Where does love live within you? Where can you most easily access joy in your body? When you attune to the peace of God that surpasses all understanding, where within you do you experience that? Maybe just choose one fruit to focus on in the practice. You can always do another fruit in your next practice. Allow yourself to breath with those feelings and sensations with the awareness that the Spirit is breathing through you as well. When you're ready to conclude this practice, end with this prayer or with one of your own.

Holy and gracious God, thank you for setting me free from what binds me. Thank you for the people you have placed in my community who have helped and continue to unbind me. Thank you for giving me strength and perseverance to both participate in my own unbinding and in the unbinding of those in my community. When I get bound up again, may your Spirit set me free. And, in this freedom, in the wholeness I experience with you, may the fruits of the Spirit grow wildly within me so that I am always fed by your love and have your love to share with those I encounter this day and every day. Amen.

BENEDICTION

May you know the love of God deep in your bones
so much so that you cannot help but love yourself.
With every breath, may you receive the love of God anew,
and may it integrate with the love that is already in your core.
May you remember each morning that you are woven together with the goodness of God,
that the fruits of the Spirit are your DNA.
May the breath of the Spirit guide you forward,
and may you have the courage to go where she leads.
May this deep and abiding love between you and God,
you and yourself,
you and your neighbors,
shine a bright light that nourishes your soul.
May the excesses of this light radiate from your being as nourishment for others.
May the love of God within you change everything about how you engage yourself, friends, family, and strangers.
This day, may you rest in the awareness that you are called to embody God's love for your neighbors, yes, and as yourself.
Amen.

APPENDIX

Practices for Embodied Grace

If we live by the Spirit, let us also be guided by the Spirit.
GALATIANS 5:25

Over the course of learning to embody grace, I have found a number of meditations, practices, and people to be extremely helpful on my journey. This appendix is to share these offerings in the event that they might assist you in your embodiment of grace as well. The first two are detailed guided meditations: *Breathing with the Spirit* and *Receiving God's Love*. You can read through them and practice in your own rhythm, or you can listen to recordings of these as you meditate. You can find recordings of these mediations on my website: www.carolinevogel.com. Following these meditations, there is a section on practices and people that I've found beneficial as well. My hope is that you engage what resonates with you and don't worry about the rest. Again, embodying grace is so much about building practices that work with the wisdom of your body, mind, and spirit. So, I encourage you to notice what works for you.

Meditation involves formal practice, which influences informal practice. In other words, when we set aside time to spend with God and attune to the breath of the Spirit who is always breathing us (formal practice), we can more easily access and be guided during the rest of our days and nights (informal practice). The formal practice of the quiet time set aside to be with God greatly impacts our ability to be with and be instructed by God throughout the rest of the day. So, start with whatever you've got—thirty seconds, three minutes, eight minutes, twenty minutes. Find a quiet place where you can just be to practice meditation—intentional time with our loving God.

Meditations

Breathing with the Spirit: A Guided Meditation

As you come to stillness, you might want to close your eyes or cast them down. This allows you to focus your attention on your inner landscape rather than staying connected to (and often distracted by) all the visual stimuli around you. As you close your eyes, you might find that you're now paying more attention to your thoughts, and that isn't very fun or desirable. You may have a sudden urge to pick up your phone, clean the bathroom, or finish an email you started eight months ago. You may want to turn your attention to anything but what's going on inside. Hang in there.

Very intentionally, invite your attention to notice the feelings and sensations in your body as your body connects with whatever is beneath and/or behind you. So, if you're lying down, notice all the points of contact along that back side of your body meeting the mat, sofa, bed, floor you're lying on. If you're in a sitting position, notice how your legs are being met by the cushion, mat, floor, chair beneath you. If you're standing, notice how your feet are connecting with the ground beneath you. Intentionally notice your feet. Notice your hands.

Now draw your attention to your breath. Notice the life-giving breath moving in and out of your body. You might want to start with your attention grounded in your nostrils. You're simply going to be aware of feelings and sensations of breath moving in and out of your nose.

When you notice that your mind drifts, try not to become stressed. That's just a mind being a mind. Kindly, gently, firmly, draw your attention back to the nose and the breath moving in and out of your body.

Next, you can drop your attention down into your chest. You might even want to put a hand on your chest. Simply notice the breath moving in and out of your chest, creating that slight rise and fall of your chest. Again, if your mind drifts, that is okay. We don't judge the heart for beating or the lungs for breathing. Use the drift as an opportunity to kindly, gently, firmly draw the attention back to the body and the breath.

After several inhalations and exhalations at the chest, you can drop the attention even further into the torso—the belly. You can place a hand on the belly if you want to. Now notice even the slightest expansion of the belly as you breathe in and deflation of the belly as you breath out. You may notice an inclination to slow the breathing down a bit to really access this belly breathing (diaphragmatic breathing). After anchoring your attention in your belly for several rounds of breathing, then you can choose where you'd like to anchor your attention—nostrils, chest, belly, or back to the connection your body is making with whatever is beneath you.

As you breathe, allow your awareness to open to how your human breath is infinitely connected to the breath of our loving God. You don't need to try and figure this out. No need to get heady about it. No analyzing. It's simply setting the intention to be open. Much like a flower opens when it blooms, imagine your awareness blooming as it opens to the wisdom that your breath is infinitely connected to a loving God. As you breathe, allow yourself to be breathed by the holy. Open to the inherent wisdom that the holy is always breathing you whether you are paying attention or not. Meditation and centering prayer is an extraordinary opportunity to come home to the wisdom that is already within us. Left to our own devices without intentional time with God, it is all too easy to bypass the reality that God is always with us, the Advocate is always breathing with us.

So, as you breathe and allow yourself to be breathed, notice any effects this has on your body. There may be no noticeable effect. Be curious about a softening and strengthening in your body as you allow yourself to be breathed by the Spirit. Allow yourself to be nourished by this holy breath. Trust that this holy breath woven with your human breath is truly sustaining you.

Notice any willingness within your being to surrender to this holy breath so that you can be guided by the Spirit. In this way, we can allow the Advocate to guide us into all truth. You may want to stay here, breathing awareness of this nurturing, sustaining, and guiding. Beautiful. When you're ready to continue, read on.

As you breathe, notice how your in-breath expands your lungs, heart, and chest. You may want to place your hand back on your chest. Register that the lungs, heart, and chest make room to receive the Spirit with every inhalation. As you exhale, imagine there is a concentration of Spirit energy in the core of your being. So, as you breathe, you're allowing the Spirit space within your being. Inhale—expansion to receive. Exhale—concentration of Spirit presence in your core. As you breathe in and out, allow this pattern of receiving and concentration of Spirit. You may want to imagine the Spirit breath has a color. Choose a color you associate with the Spirit and/or healing. As you inhale, you can see the color growing through your lungs, heart, and chest. With the exhale, you can imagine the color concentrating in the center of your chest.

Notice how this rhythm of receiving Spirit and concentration of Spirit has a way of nourishing you. As you intentionally notice the receiving and concentration, be curious about how this rhythm attunes you to the presence of the holy. Again, the Spirit is always breathing with us regardless of whether we're paying attention or not. Meditation and centering prayer become these incredible opportunities to notice and attune to what the Spirit is organically doing within us all the time. The gift of intentionally attuning to Spirit is allowing her guidance to rise in our consciousness. The more we're awake to her presence breathing within us, the easier it is to access her guidance. Whether we're meditating or moving about our days working, parenting, puttering at home, exercising, connecting with a partner, sharing with a friend, or engaging a stranger, we can access that holy breath within and be guided by her wisdom.

Now you may want to very intentionally take in holy breath with color and imagine your mind being breathed by the Spirit. Allow the breath of the Spirit to infuse any thoughts you're having. Allow the Spirit to breathe through any thought patterns of which you are aware. You may imagine the Spirit swooping in and creating a holy basin that is constantly nourishing your mind. As the Spirit breathes your mind and thoughts, see if your mind and thoughts can find some ease knowing the Spirit is breathing through them. As the Spirit breathes through your mind, notice if there is any willingness to let some thoughts ago. Allow the Spirit to sweep away any clutter within the mind. Notice a willingness to let anything and everything that doesn't serve your mind fall away by the Spirit's breath.

What would it be like to allow the Spirit to breathe through your mind before you get out of bed in the morning? How might that change the trajectory of your day? What about intentionally allowing the breath of the Spirit to breathe through your mind before you open your mouth to speak? As you listen to another speak?

After allowing the Spirit space to breathe through your mind and thoughts, very intentionally allow the breath of the Spirit to drop into your heart space. You may want to place a hand over your heart again. As you feel the slight rise and fall of your chest as you breathe, imagine the Spirit breathing your heart. Whatever you have been feeling lately or in this very moment, allow the Spirit to see those emotions and feel them with you. Recognize that you are not alone in your emotions. No matter how big or how small the emotion, the Spirit is breathing through your heart with you. Allow your heart to be just as it is while it's being breathed by the Spirit. You may imagine the Spirit's breath sweeping through your heart and brushing away anything that doesn't serve you, allowing any heart clutter to fall away with ease and leaving more room for the Spirit to breathe your heart more fully.

How does it shift things for you to realize you're not alone in your emotions? That a loving God through the breath of the Spirit is seeing you and feeling your emotions alongside you? How does it change things to allow your heart to be breathed? Do you notice any change in feeling around or in your heart? What difference does it make to allow the Spirit access to your heart?

Once you've spent some time breathing with the Spirit in your heart space, allow the Spirit to drop down into your gut. We often think of our gut as the home of intuition. You may have had a "gut feeling" about something. Sometimes, we have a knowing about something and we don't even know why or know how we know something. You may want to place a hand on your gut and just breathe. Allow room for the Spirit to breathe through your gut. Allow her to guide any sense of knowing you have or yearn to have. As the Spirit breathes through your gut, you may imagine gut clutter falling away. Anything that gets in the way of your intuition or sense of knowing, let the Spirit breathe it away.

What do you notice as you allow your gut to be breathed? Is there any greater awareness of intuition? Is there a knowing that becomes more clear? As the Spirit breathes through your intuition, do you have a sense of what is falling away? What has gotten in the way of a clear knowing previously? All these answers may not come rushing forward. Stay open. Stay curious.

As you come to the end of the meditation, allow yourself to notice how your body is making contact with whatever is beneath you—a meditation cushion, your yoga mat, the floor, your bed, the chair. Allow this mindful connection to ground you in your body. And, when you're ready, flutter your eyes open and allow your vision to integrate with the rest of your senses. Take some slow deep breaths, and with your eyes open, see if you can stay connected to a deep sense of the Spirit breathing you. It's usually so much easier to stay connected with the breath of the Spirit when we have our eyes closed. Part of the spiritual discipline is using the experience of formal practice (sitting in meditation and connecting with the breath of the Spirit) to influence our informal practice (life!).

The Spirit is always breathing us. Can we remember? Can we tap into that holy breath and allow ourselves to be guided, moment by moment, breath by breath? Imagine how life might be different if we truly allowed ourselves to be guided by the Spirit into all truth. As we move about the day, can we mindfully stay in each moment and allow the Spirit to breathe us?

Receiving God's Love: A Guided Meditation

Wherever you are on the journey of opening to God's love, see if you can sit for a bit in stillness. Eyes closed or cast down, focusing your attention again on your breath. You may want to place a hand over your heart and simply breathe with your heart. You may notice a natural inclination to slow your breathing down. Extend your inbreath and elongate your outbreath.

As you breathe slowly with your hand over your heart, see if you can sense your way down into your heart. For example, you may feel a warmth beneath your hand. Allow that warmth to lower into your heart space. Stay attuned to your breath as you train your attention on the heart itself. Sense the presence of God's love already woven within you. No need to search for it. Let the presence arise naturally beneath your hand. We are made of God's love. It is woven into every fiber and cell of our being. Meditation is a time to attune to what is already there, choosing mindfully where to place your attention (right now the heart) and breathe with the wisdom of love that abides in your heart.

As you breathe, see if you can imagine the inbreath carrying the love of God. Inhalation is about reception. On each inbreath, see if you can imagine receiving the love of God and allow that love to integrate with the love that is already there. Allow the collective love to nourish your heart. Allow your heart to be held in God's love. Can you imagine your heart being held in God's love, being breathed by the Spirit's breath?

What do you notice about your body as your heart is being held and breathed with such love? Are there feelings and sensations in your body that register a greater sense of love? Notice where that feeling congregates in your being—heart, stomach, head, arms, legs, feet? What do you notice about the heart itself? Does your heart feel different from when you first closed your eyes and began this meditation? Allow yourself to be curious about the effects God's love and the Spirit's breath have on your heart, mind, and whole body. Again, there is no force, there is no "have to," there is no "doing it right," there is no "it's supposed to feel like this." Simply allow yourself (as much as possible in this moment without force) to be breathed and to be loved. Be breathed and be loved.

Even if this exercise of meditation felt tricky in some ways, hard to connect with, or clunky, allow yourself to be mindful, curious, as open as possible to discovering God's love within you. As you move about your days, be curious how the love of God is always connecting with God's love that already exists within you. The formal practice of meditation allows us the opportunity to be with that which is already there, yet we rarely, if ever, give ourselves time and space to experience God's love within. The Spirit can be a grounding force in our everyday lives. When we spend this precious time intentionally dwelling in the love of God and breath of the Spirit, it can change our hearts and our lives. The informal meditation called life can be greatly impacted by both the time we spend in formal meditation with the breath of the Spirit and love of God *and* how we train our mind as we move through our days. Formal meditation yoked with informal mindfulness can change how we experience ourselves and the world around us. When we are strongly anchored in the inner love of God, our hearts, our minds, and bodies move through the world differently. We have an easier time not only embodying the love of God but all the gifts of the Spirit. We are intentional vessels of God's love.

Floating Outside the "Christian" Channels—Modalities that Assist in Embodying Grace

I've gained a great deal of learning and wisdom by intentionally floating outside the traditional Christian channels and boxes. What follows are brief descriptions of some of the practices and experiences that have been most meaningful to me on this journey of loving myself. Over and over again, through these classes and courses that have proven to be endlessly healing and helpful to millions of people, I've found the Holy Spirit teaching me something new about my Christian faith. Each tool acquired offered a way home to a loving God within, a greater capacity to live my faith moment by moment, and a widening ability to both receive and share the fruits of the Spirit and stay in her flow.

Mindfulness-Based Stress Reduction (MBSR)

The mindfulness-based stress reduction (MBSR) course created by Jon Kabat-Zinn more than thirty years ago taught me how to meditate and helped me understand how my body and mind work together (or don't work together) under stress. Though a clearly secular offering, MBSR opened the door for me to learn to be still so that I could better appreciate that God was God and that God was with me. It has assisted me in the embodiment of "be still and know that I am God." It also created the opportunity for me to notice the feelings and sensations in my body moment by moment, which cracked the window to truly seeing my body as a temple of the Holy Spirit.

If I stay attuned to the feelings and sensations in my body, I can better connect with the wisdom God has woven into my being. The Spirit is constantly breathing through this wisdom. The stillness of meditation allows me to not only come home to the wisdom of knowing God is God, it also opens the pathway to experience the inherent wisdom with which we are woven together. Our bodies are indeed temples for the breath of the Spirit to breathe into, as well as reservoirs of inherent wisdom.

Mindful-Self Compassion (MSC)

A course on Mindful Self-Compassion (MSC) created by Kristin Neff and Chris Gerber began to enlighten my mind and stir my heart to the true meaning of compassion and how one might practice compassion with oneself. Compassion is turning toward pain and suffering with love and kindness, ease and gentleness. Many Christians are good at turning toward others with compassion but lack the capacity or maybe even the permission to turn toward their own pain and suffering. As I studied and began to practice MSC, the eyes of my heart enlightened to how Jesus speaks to me, as opposed to the fierce critic I find in my mind waiting to pounce on any given action, word, or inaction. MSC taught me to shift from self-judgment to self-compassion, which was a huge boost to my ability to embody grace within my mind.

One of the many resources that has helped me to better understand, appreciate, and embody gentleness along with love, peace, patience, kindness, and generosity toward myself and others is the practice of MSC. Neff and Germer have a great deal to teach about this approach to meditation and life. There is a great misconception that we have to be hard on ourselves to get things done or be successful. I always knew I had been hard on myself but it wasn't until engaging this curriculum and practice that I realized just how much I believed the inner critic was necessary to achieve in life and maybe even survive on some level. For anyone wanting to learn more and grow in your capacity to be gentle with yourself, I highly recommend looking into Mindful Self-Compassion.

Emotional Brain Training (EBT)

The insight of Laurel Mellin's Emotional Brain Training (EBT) gave me tools to process my feelings in ways that allowed me to both feel them and move through them so as not to get stuck. EBT offers the opportunity to process what I previously wanted to deny or numb so that I can create resiliency and stay in the flow of the Holy Spirit. Prior to this learning, I had a pattern of getting stuck in my mind and allowing my emotion to get lodged in my body, which makes it quite difficult to stay in the flow of the Holy Spirit.

Eye Movement Desensitization Reprocessing (EMDR)

The therapeutic modality of EMDR (Eye Movement Desensitization Reprocessing) helps to clear stress and trauma from recent events and to clear the buildup of stress and trauma through the years. Though meditation, mindful self-compassion, and EBT can be practiced alone, EMDR must be practiced with a skilled EMDR therapist. Sometimes pathways are blocked from years of stress responses. Pathways are blocked because they've never had the opportunity to process stressful or traumatic material in healthy ways. EMDR is a modality used now to help people process what has remained stuck and frees them to lead healthier, happier, more whole lives. From this place of being unstuck, one has such a greater capacity to connect with the flow of the Spirit and embody meaningful grace.

Working with Others to Address What Gets in the Way of Embodying Grace

If embodying God's love, living in the breath of the Spirit, and sharing the Spirit's fruits were easy, we'd already be doing it with ease by now. We've already acknowledged that the stress and trauma of life often cover up our DNA goodness: we cannot just take a Clorox wipe and scrub away the buildup of stress and trauma. Wouldn't that be grand if we could?

Throughout the book, I have provided spiritual practices that can assist us in sweeping away the stress and toxicity that pile up so that we can live more aligned with the Spirit goodness within us. But this work doesn't have to happen on our own. What follows are some descriptions of relationships that you might find helpful as you prayerfully begin and/or continue to embody God's grace.

Anam Caras

An *anam cara* is a soul friend. I've been blessed with a couple of women in my life over the years who have genuinely felt like soul friends. Each of my *anam caras* has been more than a friend. Yes, we can talk about the weather or parenting, relationships or cooking ideas, but what marks these soulful connections is just that—to connect with each other's soul in the benevolence of the divine.

Each of these women is faithful and steadfast in her own spiritual life in addition to being a good caretaker of her own emotional and mental health. When we get together, there is a sharing from the depth of our beings. We share from where the Spirit breathes through us. It is in these sacred friendships that I can really let down my guard and have the space to be as raw and vulnerable as I need or want to be without fear and trepidation of how what I share might be used or called forth at another time. I pray for these friends and their soulful paths, and they pray for mine. We experience a kind of radical being for each other. There is some kind of soulful recognition that the evolution of my soul encourages the evolution of her soul and vice versa. As we encourage one another and cheer each other on, there is a palpable sense that the Spirit is breathing through each other. Somehow their encouragement carries the blessing of the holy.

You cannot orchestrate these friendships. I've never been able to go out and find them. Pray for them, yes. In each case, they have proven to be more fulfilling, kind, and full of grace than I could have known to pray for, and for that, I will always be grateful. When they come around for however long, I have learned to very intentionally turn to God and say *thank you*. Then I keep saying thank you. I've had to learn to hold *anam caras* lightly and loosely as my natural tendency is to want to hold on to them for dear life. The friendship itself is woven of the Spirit, breathed by the Spirit, and enlightened by the Spirit. These friendships are to be trusted in the Spirit. I'm deeply grateful for how the *anam caras* in my life have greatly assisted me in my ability to receive grace, share God's love, and embody the gifts of the Spirit. My life is ever better, richer for them.

Spiritual Companionship

Sometimes we need people to very intentionally hold space with us. We need a palpable sense of being with someone as we discern the will of God, the breath of the Spirit, the light of Christ, the movement of the holy, and the presence of love. Spiritual companions are trained to hold sacred space with others. Most people called to this shared space have an intuitive ability to listen for the Spirit with people. This practice used to be called spiritual direction. I have stopped using that term as I never felt like a director in this role. I always felt the Spirit was and is the director in spiritual direction, and that I was called to be a companion along the way for someone. Spiritual companions don't (or rarely) give advice. They are there to help you hear your own soul better and to discern the presence of our loving God in all aspects of your life (or whatever aspects you want to bring to the table).

Oftentimes, people seek out spiritual companionship because they are feeling stuck in their lives—stuck in their faith, stuck in their spiritual practices, stuck in their relationship to their church or community, stuck in their relationship with God, stuck in how they are relating to themselves, stuck in their vocation, or stuck in their key relationships. They come looking for a place to process this stuckness and find healthy ways forward guided by the Spirit.

I've always found the spiritual life a humbling path—likely by divine design. As much as I have wanted to be able to intuit and discern the will of God, receive the love of God, breathe with the Spirit and embody her gifts, I have not been able to figure out any of this alone. I've needed companions along the way. Some have been friends, some *anam caras*, and some spiritual companions. There is something deeply sacred about really allowing someone to journey alongside you as you intentionally live your faith and/or follow the Spirit.

Therapists

Not everyone who engages the spiritual path needs therapy or counseling. However, there are times when neither an *anam cara* nor a spiritual companion has the skills, time, energy, or capacity to engage the blocks with which you might be dealing. Both little "t" traumas and big "T" traumas can leave lasting effects on the body, mind, and heart that make it difficult to access the love of God within us. The issues that get stuck in our tissues make it difficult to embody the fruits of the Spirit or even breathe with the Spirit. If you are feeling stuck in your spiritual life and/or experiencing anxiety, depression, over-worrying, and stress responses that get in the way, you might want to reach out to a therapist. The best way to find a good therapist in your area is word of mouth. Ask trusted friends, colleagues, mentors, or your physician for someone they would recommend.